SpringerBriefs in Computer Science

SpringerBriefs present concise summaries of cutting-edge research and practical applications across a wide spectrum of fields. Featuring compact volumes of 50 to 125 pages, the series covers a range of content from professional to academic.

Typical topics might include:

- A timely report of state-of-the art analytical techniques
- A bridge between new research results, as published in journal articles, and a contextual literature review
- A snapshot of a hot or emerging topic
- An in-depth case study or clinical example
- A presentation of core concepts that students must understand in order to make independent contributions

Briefs allow authors to present their ideas and readers to absorb them with minimal time investment. Briefs will be published as part of Springer's eBook collection, with millions of users worldwide. In addition, Briefs will be available for individual print and electronic purchase. Briefs are characterized by fast, global electronic dissemination, standard publishing contracts, easy-to-use manuscript preparation and formatting guidelines, and expedited production schedules. We aim for publication 8–12 weeks after acceptance. Both solicited and unsolicited manuscripts are considered for publication in this series.

More information about this series at http://www.springer.com/series/10028

Sandeep Kumar · Niyati Baliyan

Semantic Web-Based Systems

Quality Assessment Models

 Springer

Sandeep Kumar
Department of Computer Science and
  Engineering
Indian Institute of Technology Roorkee
Roorkee, Uttarakhand
India

Niyati Baliyan
Department of Information Technology
Indira Gandhi Delhi Technical University for
  Women
New Delhi, Delhi
India

ISSN 2191-5768   ISSN 2191-5776   (electronic)
SpringerBriefs in Computer Science
ISBN 978-981-10-7699-2   ISBN 978-981-10-7700-5   (eBook)
https://doi.org/10.1007/978-981-10-7700-5

Library of Congress Control Number: 2018945453

Printed on acid-free paper

This Springer imprint is published by the registered company Springer Nature Singapore Pte Ltd.
The registered company address is: 152 Beach Road, #21-01/04 Gateway East, Singapore 189721, Singapore

Preface

As a result of dynamic nature of software, the software engineering study and practice has transformed drastically. There have been transitions from a stand-alone application to Web application and a recent development being that of Semantic Web-based applications. Semantic Web is characterized by machine comprehensibility of the content, sharing, and reuse among heterogeneous applications, modular structure of its domain vocabulary, and availability as a service. Owing to the difference in characteristics of such applications, the currently available software quality models are considered to be either inappropriate or incomplete for the assessment of Semantic Web-based applications. Quality evaluation of Semantic Web-based applications is an interesting problem nowadays since they are not solely utilized for information retrieval in a semantic search engine, but being widely employed in the healthcare industry, social networks, e-learning programs, and multimedia processing, among others. Semantic Web applications are a layered cake with ontology at the backbone, description and formal logic in the middle, and the deployment layer at the outermost end. Further, the syntactical composition of ontology as well as its behavior within a Semantic Web-based system or application needs to be assessed. This book initially presents the basic concepts related to the Semantic Web, Semantic Web-based applications, Web applications, ontology and their quality aspects. In addition to various important works reported in this area, our reported works on evaluating the structural quality of modular ontologies and additionally metrics for evaluation of ontology behavior are also summarized. In the presence of multiple Semantic Web applications, offering similar functionality, it is reasonable to evaluate them and make a choice based on the fulfillment of non-functional requirements from them. Further, the quality evaluation of Semantic Web applications deployed on the cloud is summarized, in order to better understand, maintain, integrate, and reuse such applications. This book has been organized as follows. Chapter 1 provides a brief introduction to some of the basic topics related to Semantic Web, ontology, modular ontology, quality, etc. Chapter 2 presents quality assessment of modular ontology. The chapter initially summarizes some works reported in this direction and then discusses one of the models in detail. Chapter 3 discusses the quality evaluation of Semantic Web-based applications as a whole. Chapter 4 provides a discussion on quality evaluation of Semantic Web applications deployed as service. The primary contribution of this book lies in presenting a single source of information for software engineers in general and ontology engineers in particular in figuring out the best modularization on the basis of goodness of (re)use, irrespective of their types and size. This book can also work as an initial source of information for starting research in this domain. We are hopeful that this book will not only provide a good introductory reference but also give the reader a breadth and depth of this topic.

Roorkee, India   Sandeep Kumar
New Delhi, India   Niyati Baliyan

Acknowledgements

I would like to express my sincere thanks to my institute, Indian Institute of Technology Roorkee, India, for providing me healthy and conducive working environment. I am also thankful to the faculty members of the Department of Computer Science and Engineering, Indian Institute of Technology Roorkee, India, for their constant support and encouragement. I am especially thankful to some of my colleagues there, who are more like friends and give me constant support. I am thankful to my past postgraduate students, especially Shriya Sukalikar and Satish Dalal, whose work helped in some part of this book. I am also thankful to Prof. R. B. Mishra of Indian Institute of Technology, Banaras Hindu University, India, for his guidance. I am also grateful to the editor and the publication team of the Springer. I am really thankful to my wife, sisters, brother, parents-in-law, and my lovely daughter Aastha, who is my life, for their love and blessings. I have no words to mention the support, patience, and sacrifice of my parents. I dedicate this book to God and to my family.

—Sandeep Kumar

I express profound gratitude to God. I also feel extremely thankful to a lot of people who facilitated the start and finish of this book, either directly or indirectly. I thank Dr. Sandeep Kumar, first and foremost for the impetus to write this book. I want to acknowledge my husband for his persistent backing. It is also hard to imagine this book without the blessing of my parents. I thank all my friends and colleagues for being a source of inspiration and love throughout my journey. I want to thank anonymous reviewers for proofreading the chapters and the publishing team.

—Niyati Baliyan

Contents

About the Authors

Sandeep Kumar (SMIEEE'17) is currently working as an assistant professor in the Department of Computer Science and Engineering, Indian Institute of Technology (IIT) Roorkee, India. He has supervised three Ph.D. theses, about 30 master dissertations, about 15 undergraduate projects and is currently supervising four Ph.D. students. He has published more than 45 research papers in international/ national journals and conferences and has also written books/chapters with Springer, USA, and IGI Publications, USA. He has also filed two patents for his work done along with his students. He is the member of the board of examiners and board of studies of various universities and institutions. He has collaborations in industry and academia. He is currently handling multiple national and international research/ consultancy projects. He has received NSF/TCPP early adopter award-2014, 2015, ITS Travel Award 2011 and 2013, and others. He is the member of ACM and senior member of IEEE. His name has also been enlisted in major directories such as Marquis Who's Who, IBC. His areas of interest include Semantic Web, Web services, and software engineering. Email: sandeepkumargarg@gmail.com, sgargfec@iitr.ac.in

Niyati Baliyan received her Ph.D. degree from the Computer Science and Engineering Department, Indian Institute of Technology Roorkee, India, in 2016. She topped Gautam Buddha University, Greater Noida, India, during her M.Tech. program in Information and Communication Technology. She has also attained post-graduate certificate with honors in Information Technology from Sheffield Hallam University, UK, where she was an exchange student on scholarship. She has authored and reviewed many chapters, journals, and conference papers. She is currently working as an assistant professor at Indira Gandhi Delhi Technical University for Women, New Delhi, Delhi, India. Prior to this, she has guided four M.E. theses while teaching at Thapar Institute of Engineering and Technology University, Patiala, India. Her research interests include Semantic Web, ontologies, graph theory, and data analytics. Email: niyati.baliyan@gmail.com, niyatibaliyan@igdtuw.ac.in

Chapter 1
Introduction

Abstract The conventional software has traversed a long route from a stand-alone application to a Web application, and now Semantic Web application, sometimes deployed as a service. In parallel, software engineering has evolved significantly in the recent years, with respect to the way it is studied as well as the way it is practiced. This change can majorly be attributed to the constantly changing characteristics of software. The machine-comprehendible, sharable, reusable content across multiple applications, modular structure of domain-specific vocabulary (ontology), and availability of the application as a service may be cited as a few factors for the popular use of Semantic Web-based applications. As reflected in their name, Semantic Web-based applications render meaningful information or knowledge to their users, at the time of storage and retrieval. However, nowadays, these applications are not merely used for information retrieval through a semantic search engine; they have rather found a viable marketplace in the healthcare industry, social networks, e-learning platforms, and multimedia processing, to name a few. Semantic Web research prototypes are now prevalent and gain the interest of academicians, owing to the knowledge contained in them in the form of a modularly structured vocabulary of a particular domain, namely ontology. When annotated to an application, ontology serves as metadata and makes the application more meaningful and hence more powerful. It is said that what cannot be measured, cannot be improved, hence the motivation to measure the quality of Semantic Web applications to exploit them for effective use. The notion of quality is primarily concerned with the satisfaction of explicit and implicit needs of the users of the entity whose quality is in question. The software quality models available as on date are found to be either incomplete or irrelevant for the evaluation of Semantic Web-based applications. A quality framework for the Semantic Web applications will acknowledge their layered structure; there is ontology at the bottom, description logic in the middle, and deployment layer at the top. The quality assessment of Semantic Web applications at various layers may give various perspectives to the developers as well as to the users and assist them in conforming to and confirming quality, respectively.

Keywords Semantic Web · Ontology · Quality

© The Author(s) 2018
S. Kumar and N. Baliyan, *Semantic Web-Based Systems*, SpringerBriefs in Computer Science, https://doi.org/10.1007/978-981-10-7700-5_1

This chapter introduces primary topics of the book, i.e., Semantic Web, ontology, and quality, along with mentioning relevant terminology used throughout the book. This chapter is organized as follows. Section 1.1 presents the fundamentals of Semantic Web along with its layered architecture. A discussion on ontology in the purview of modular ontology is given in Sect. 1.2. Next, Sect. 1.3 gives an overview of the software evolution, jotting down striking differences among conventional and contemporary Web applications, and Semantic Web applications. Section 1.4 briefly discusses Semantic Web applications when deployed on the cloud, i.e., as a service. The notion of quality is presented in Sect. 1.5. Lastly, Sect. 1.6 concludes this introductory chapter.

1.1 Semantic Web

The idea of Semantic Web has emerged from the project of Berners-Lee et al. (2001), who anticipated a Web of data. In other words, Berners-Lee envisioned Web in the form of one unified storehouse of information instead of a massive pool of Web sites and Web pages. Semantic Web is not a substitute for, rather an addition to the current Web. The Semantic Web enables information to have clearly defined meaning, thereby facilitating computer and people to work in collaboration. Both machines and humans can infer the meaning on the Semantic Web, with the intention of sharing, reusing, searching, and aggregating Web's information. This is made feasible through addition of new data and metadata to existing Web documents. The Semantic Web achieves the primary goal of advanced automatic processing of Web contents by man and machine alike, by building a layer on the current Web.

The Semantic Web uses the notion of self-describing, machine-understandable knowledge, which is accessible through standard Web-programming constructs. The semantic layer links numerous knowledge sources carrying well-defined semantics, across the Web (Schwartz 2003). Semantic Web attempts to capture and make use of content's semantics in order to renovate current Web from a platform for information representation to a platform for information comprehension and reasoning (McGuinness et al. 2002). With trillion Web sites in place, and billions of users, the Semantic Web technology clearly enables a smarter search instead of string matching, query response instead of information retrieval, document exchange across heterogeneous sources via ontology mappings, and definition of tailored views on documents (Fensel 2005). Furthermore, semantic annotations in Web services may automate service discovery, composition, negotiation, and delivery.

The Semantic Web is no longer merely a vision, the Semantic Web technology is widely being used in real-world applications such as Twine, Swoogle, Freebase, Google Knowledge Graph, Mozilla Firefox (Floridi 2009), and its applications have been reported in various works (Iribarne et al. 2011; Asensio et al. 2011; Smith et al. 2014). The advantages of this Web of data over conventional Web are many: improved searches, faster retrieval, and handling of an average query, particularly in a data-centric domain, to name a few. Imagine that a patient's medical history, despite being procured from multiple heterogeneous sources, can be organized, sifted, and reused by a doctor if it is given in the hands of Semantic Web technologies. For fulfilling this functional requirement, a Semantic Web-based application can be developed in the field of health care, reaping numerous benefits such as enhanced productivity, decreased development time and cost, and improved quality. Antoniou and Harmelen (2004) define some terms relevant in the context of Semantic Web as follows:

- Resource: anything that the Uniform Resource Indicator (URI) can identify.
- Language: means to formal specification, could be parsing or processing.
- Semantic Annotations: metadata describing an object and its property value or two objects and their relation in a formal way. Some languages for semantic annotations are Resource Description Framework (RDF), Web Ontology Language (OWL), etc. The annotations can be manual or automatic.
- RDF represents metadata in the form of triplets <object, property, value> or <object, relation, object>.
- Ontology: vocabulary of a domain, often represented as a graph for annotation.
- Logical support: rules to infer explicit content from implicit content (i.e., meaning from semantic annotations and ontology). The language for rules is Rule Modeling Language (RuleML). Its tools are called knowledge acquisition tools.
- SPARQL Protocol and RDF Query Language (SPARQL) verify structured data.

The context-specific taxonomy and related constraints are structured data, which is machine understandable, expressed in OWL, and verified in SPARQL (Antoniou et al. 2012). Figure 1.1 illustrates the interlocking ideas of HTML, RDF, and metadata.

Fig. 1.1 RDF and structured
data

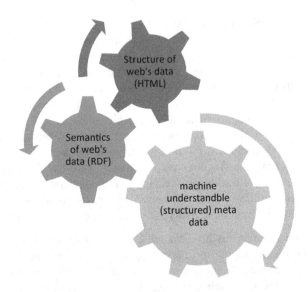

With the advent of Semantic Web, both users and machines act as producers and consumers of data and documents carry semantic annotations. The Semantic Web is also known as Web 3.0 as opposed to Web 2.0 where there were documents and users; the latter act as both producer and consumer of data. Even much earlier, the Web 1.0 comprised dedicated users as producers and consumers of data, in a mutually exclusive fashion.

1.1.1 Layered Architecture of Semantic Web

The Semantic Web architecture can be viewed as a layered stack of technologies (Fugini et al. 2016). As seen in Fig. 1.2, at the bottom there is URI as a string of characters for the identification of a name or a resource. The RDF is a generic way of modeling Web resource information, with the help of syntactic formatting. The Extensible Markup Language (XML) draws rules for encoding documents in a human- and machine-understandable format. On the top of RDF/XML is the RDF schema, which is a collection of classes with specific features for describing ontologies. Each language for the Semantic Web (such as OWL) gives a formal meaning based on model-theoretic semantics in its abstract syntax. The unifying logic and proof establish truth of statements and infer unstated facts. Right beneath the outermost layer of user interface and Semantic Web applications is the trust, signifying authentication of statements.

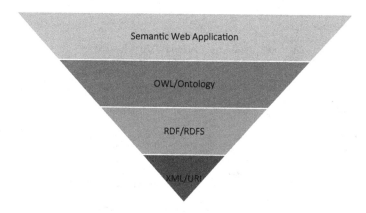

Fig. 1.2 Partial layers in a Semantic Web application

1.2 Ontology

Ontology is a group of descriptive primitives, which represents knowledge of a particular domain and forms an elementary unit of inference techniques on the Semantic Web (Gruber 2009). Hence, it is crucial to assess the quality of ontologies in order for users to better understand, maintain, reuse, and integrate ontologies. Chapter 2 discusses this in detail.

Ontology is an explicit, formal specification of a shared conceptualization. (Gruber 1993)

In this definition, *explicit* means that the ontology concepts and their usage constraints are explicitly defined. *Formal* means that the ontology should be machine understandable. *Shared* means that an ontology is not confined to an individual but recognized by a group. *Conceptualization* refers to an abstract model of some phenomenon in the world that identifies the pertinent concepts of that phenomenon (Gruber 1993). Ontologies provide a shared understanding of a domain that enables to overcome the variances in vocabulary on the Web. Thus, ontologies can be used to provide semantic interoperability (Thomasson 2014). Some formal languages called ontology languages can encode ontologies. Examples of such languages are: RDF, RDF-S, OWL, OWL-S. An ontology excerpt for the ontology used in the work of Baliyan and Kumar (2016a) is presented below.

```
"…..
  <?xml version="1.0"?>
  <!DOCTYPE Ontology [
      <!ENTITY xsd "http://www.w3.org/2001/XMLSchema#" >
      <!ENTITY xml "http://www.w3.org/XML/1998/namespace" >
      <!ENTITY rdfs "http://www.w3.org/2000/01/rdf-schema#" >
      <!ENTITY rdf "http://www.w3.org/1999/02/22-rdf-syntax-ns#" >
  ]>
  <Ontology xmlns="http://www.w3.org/2002/07/owl#"

xml:base="http://www.semanticweb.org/admin/ontologies/2014/4/areasOntology"
      xmlns:rdfs="http://www.w3.org/2000/01/rdf-schema#"
      xmlns:xsd="http://www.w3.org/2001/XMLSchema#"
      xmlns:rdf="http://www.w3.org/1999/02/22-rdf-syntax-ns#"
      xmlns:xml="http://www.w3.org/XML/1998/namespace"

ontologyIRI="http://www.semanticweb.org/admin/ontologies/2014/4/areasOntology
">
      <Prefix name="" IRI="http://www.w3.org/2002/07/owl#"/>
      <Prefix name="owl" IRI="http://www.w3.org/2002/07/owl#"/>
      <Prefix name="rdf" IRI="http://www.w3.org/1999/02/22-rdf-syntax-ns#"/>
      <Prefix name="xsd" IRI="http://www.w3.org/2001/XMLSchema#"/>
      <Prefix name="rdfs" IRI="http://www.w3.org/2000/01/rdf-schema#"/>
      <Declaration>
          <Class
IRI="http://www.semanticweb.org/admin/ontologies/2014/4/untitled-ontology-
20#City"/>
      </Declaration>
      <Declaration>
          <Class
IRI="http://www.semanticweb.org/admin/ontologies/2014/4/untitled-ontology-
20#Country"/>
      </Declaration>
      <Declaration>
          <Class
IRI="http://www.semanticweb.org/admin/ontologies/2014/4/untitled-ontology-
20#Place"/>
      </Declaration>
      <Declaration>
          <Class
IRI="http://www.semanticweb.org/admin/ontologies/2014/4/untitled-ontology-
20#State"/>
      </Declaration>
      <Declaration>
          <ObjectProperty
IRI="http://www.semanticweb.org/admin/ontologies/2014/4/untitled-ontology-
20#borders"/>
      </Declaration>
```

```
        <Declaration>
            <ObjectProperty
IRI="http://www.semanticweb.org/admin/ontologies/2014/4/untitled-ontology-
20#isCapitalOf"/>
        </Declaration>
        <Declaration>
            <ObjectProperty
IRI="http://www.semanticweb.org/admin/ontologies/2014/4/untitled-ontology-
20#isLocatedIn"/>
        </Declaration>
        <Declaration>
            <ObjectProperty
IRI="http://www.semanticweb.org/admin/ontologies/2014/4/untitled-ontology-
20#isPartOf"/>
        </Declaration>
        <Declaration>
            <DataProperty
IRI="http://www.semanticweb.org/admin/ontologies/2014/4/untitled-ontology-
20#population"/>
        </Declaration>
        <SubClassOf>
            <Class
IRI="http://www.semanticweb.org/admin/ontologies/2014/4/untitled-ontology-
20#City"/>
            <Class
IRI="http://www.semanticweb.org/admin/ontologies/2014/4/untitled-ontology-
20#Place"/>
        </SubClassOf>
        <SubClassOf>
            <Class
IRI="http://www.semanticweb.org/admin/ontologies/2014/4/untitled-ontology-
20#Country"/>
            <Class
IRI="http://www.semanticweb.org/admin/ontologies/2014/4/untitled-ontology-
20#Place"/>
        </SubClassOf>
        <SubClassOf>
            <Class
IRI="http://www.semanticweb.org/admin/ontologies/2014/4/untitled-ontology-
20#State"/>
            <Class
IRI="http://www.semanticweb.org/admin/ontologies/2014/4/untitled-ontology-
20#Place"/>
        </SubClassOf>
        <SubObjectPropertyOf>
            <ObjectProperty
IRI="http://www.semanticweb.org/admin/ontologies/2014/4/untitled-ontology-
20#isCapitalOf"/>
```

```
        <ObjectProperty
IRI="http://www.semanticweb.org/admin/ontologies/2014/4/untitled-ontology-
20#isLocatedIn"/>
      </SubObjectPropertyOf>
      <ObjectPropertyDomain>
        <ObjectProperty
IRI="http://www.semanticweb.org/admin/ontologies/2014/4/untitled-ontology-
20#isLocatedIn"/>
        <Class
IRI="http://www.semanticweb.org/admin/ontologies/2014/4/untitled-ontology-
20#City"/>
      </ObjectPropertyDomain>
      <ObjectPropertyDomain>
        <ObjectProperty
IRI="http://www.semanticweb.org/admin/ontologies/2014/4/untitled-ontology-
20#isPartOf"/>
        <Class
IRI="http://www.semanticweb.org/admin/ontologies/2014/4/untitled-ontology-
20#State"/>
      </ObjectPropertyDomain>
      <ObjectPropertyRange>
        <ObjectProperty
IRI="http://www.semanticweb.org/admin/ontologies/2014/4/untitled-ontology-
20#isLocatedIn"/>
        <Class
IRI="http://www.semanticweb.org/admin/ontologies/2014/4/untitled-ontology-
20#Country"/>
      </ObjectPropertyRange>
      <ObjectPropertyRange>
        <ObjectProperty
IRI="http://www.semanticweb.org/admin/ontologies/2014/4/untitled-ontology-
20#isPartOf"/>
        <Class
IRI="http://www.semanticweb.org/admin/ontologies/2014/4/untitled-ontology-
20#Country"/>
      </ObjectPropertyRange>
      <DataPropertyDomain>
        <DataProperty
IRI="http://www.semanticweb.org/admin/ontologies/2014/4/untitled-ontology-
20#population"/>
        <Class
IRI="http://www.semanticweb.org/admin/ontologies/2014/4/untitled-ontology-
20#Place"/>
      </DataPropertyDomain>
      <DataPropertyRange>
        <DataProperty
IRI="http://www.semanticweb.org/admin/ontologies/2014/4/untitled-ontology-
20#population"/>
          <Datatype abbreviatedIRI="xsd:integer"/>
```

```
        </DataPropertyRange>
        <AnnotationAssertion>
            <AnnotationProperty abbreviatedIRI="rdfs:comment"/>
            <IRI>http://www.semanticweb.org/admin/ontologies/2014/4/untitled-
ontology-20#City</IRI>
            <Literal datatypeIRI="&rdf;PlainLiteral">Class of all
cities.</Literal>
        </AnnotationAssertion>
        <AnnotationAssertion>
            <AnnotationProperty abbreviatedIRI="rdfs:comment"/>
            <IRI>http://www.semanticweb.org/admin/ontologies/2014/4/untitled-
ontology-20#Country</IRI>
            <Literal datatypeIRI="&rdf;PlainLiteral">Class of all
countries.</Literal>
        </AnnotationAssertion>
        <AnnotationAssertion>
            <AnnotationProperty abbreviatedIRI="rdfs:comment"/>
            <IRI>http://www.semanticweb.org/admin/ontologies/2014/4/untitled-
ontology-20#State</IRI>
            <Literal datatypeIRI="&rdf;PlainLiteral">Class of all
states.</Literal>
        </AnnotationAssertion>
        <AnnotationAssertion>
            <AnnotationProperty abbreviatedIRI="rdfs:comment"/>
            <IRI>http://www.semanticweb.org/admin/ontologies/2014/4/untitled-
ontology-20#borders</IRI>
            <Literal datatypeIRI="&rdf;PlainLiteral">borders have domain Country
and range Country
  A country borders another country</Literal>
        </AnnotationAssertion>
        <AnnotationAssertion>
            <AnnotationProperty abbreviatedIRI="rdfs:comment"/>
            <IRI>http://www.semanticweb.org/admin/ontologies/2014/4/untitled-
ontology-20#isCapitalOf</IRI>
    <Literal datatypeIRI="&rdf;PlainLiteral">Inherits domain and range from
isLocatedIn

    </Literal>
        </AnnotationAssertion>    <AnnotationAssertion>
            <AnnotationProperty abbreviatedIRI="rdfs:comment"/>
            <IRI>http://www.semanticweb.org/admin/ontologies/2014/4/untitled-
ontology-20#isLocatedIn</IRI>
            <Literal datatypeIRI="&rdf;PlainLiteral">City &lt;isLocatedIn&gt;
Country</Literal>
        </AnnotationAssertion>    <AnnotationAssertion>
            <AnnotationProperty abbreviatedIRI="rdfs:comment"/>
            <IRI>http://www.semanticweb.org/admin/ontologies/2014/4/untitled-
ontology-20#population</IRI>
            <Literal datatypeIRI="&rdf;PlainLiteral">population has domain Place
and range integer
    </Literal>
    </AnnotationAssertion>
    </Ontology>
    …."
```

1.2.1   Modular Ontology

Ontologies may be classified as monolithic and modular, the former having limited scalability, which makes it difficult to reuse concepts. Moreover, the reasoning performance degrades while working with large and complex monolithic ontologies (Ensan and Du 2013). A modular ontology may have multiple partitions or modules characterized by high cohesion among classes within a module (Bateman et al. 2007). Hence, a modular ontology with superior quality would be easy to scale, manage, and reuse (Dalal et al. 2015). Noy et al. (2006) argue that collaboratively creating individual modules that can later be incorporated into a single ontology leads to easy management of the modules as well as better accuracy of their design.

Let us look at the ontology-related definitions by Briand et al. (1996). An ontology O is denoted as a pair $\langle C, L \rangle$ where C is a set of concepts of ontology, and L is a binary link on C ($L \subseteq C \times C$), called object property, or a link between an element of C and a datatype, called data property. In Sukalikar et al. (2014) and Kumar et al. (2017), the ontology modules have been represented using graph theoretical approach, since it suits several abstract depictions of ontologies visualized in the form of vertices and edges.

Similarly, in Fig. 1.3, ontology O is defined as: $\langle \{1, 2, 3, 4, 5, 6, 7, 8\}, \{\langle 1, 3 \rangle, \langle 1, 5 \rangle, \langle 1, 7 \rangle, \langle 4, 7 \rangle, \langle 6, 2 \rangle, \langle 6, 5 \rangle, \langle 8, 5 \rangle\} \rangle$. It has eight concepts (1–8), seven links, and two modules (m_1 and m_2).

Fig. 1.3 A modular ontology

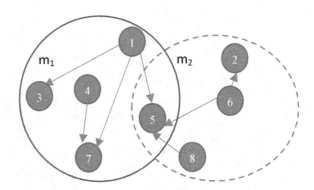

For an ontology $O = \langle C, L \rangle$, an ontology $O = \langle C_0, L_0 \rangle$ is a module of O iff $C_0 \subseteq C$, $L_0 \subseteq C_0 \times C_0$, and $L_0 \subseteq L$. In Fig. 1.3, consider the following modules:

- $m_1 = \langle C_{m_1}, L_{m_1} \rangle = \langle \{1, 3, 4, 5, 7\}, \{\langle 1, 3 \rangle, \langle 4, 7 \rangle, \langle 1, 7 \rangle, \langle 1, 5 \rangle\} \rangle$
- $m_2 = \langle C_{m_2}, L_{m_2} \rangle = \langle \{2, 5, 6, 8\}, \{\langle 6, 5 \rangle, \langle 8, 5 \rangle, \langle 6, 2 \rangle\} \rangle$

Module $m_i = \langle C_i, L_i \rangle$ is said to be included in module $m_j = \langle C_j, L_j \rangle$ (i.e., $m_i \subseteq m_j$) if $C_{m_i} \subseteq C_{m_j}$ and $L_{m_i} \subseteq L_{m_j}$. The union of modules $m_i = \langle C_i, L_i \rangle$ and $m_j = \langle C_j, L_j \rangle$ (i.e., $m_i \cup m_j$) is the module $\langle C_{m_i} \cup C_{m_j}, L_{m_i} \cup L_{m_j} \rangle$. The intersection of modules $m_i = \langle C_i, L_i \rangle$ and $m_j = \langle C_j, L_j \rangle$ (i.e., $m_i \cap m_j$) is the module $\langle C_{m_i} \cap C_{m_j}, L_{m_i} \cap L_{m_j} \rangle$. Complement of a set A is denoted by A^C. Modules m_i and m_j are said to be disjoint if $m_i \cap m_j = \varphi$ (Kumar et al. 2017).

1.3 Semantic Web Applications

Web-based applications that utilize state-of-the-art principles and technologies of the Semantic Web are Semantic Web applications (SWAs). They store, retrieve, use, and publish data in a Semantic Web format such as RDF and OWL (Berners-Lee et al. 2001). Software application and the underlying ontology are two main components of a SWA. Semantic Web technology-based Web applications are rapidly increasing and are finding usage in various domains such as information retrieval in a semantic search engine, healthcare industry, social networks, e-learning platforms, multimedia processing, etc. (Blomqvist 2014). Hence, similar to software's and Web application's quality assessment, quality assessment of Semantic Web applications is significant. Chapter 3 discusses this concept in detail.

It is due to machine comprehensible metadata, openness, computational complexity, uncertainty in Web semantics, and tractability that there is no need of human operator for adding data and metadata to documents. In order to leverage the benefits of interoperability, reusability, and thus increased productivity, it is important to monitor and improve the quality of SWAs.

1.3.1 Conventional Software Versus Web Applications

Some characteristics of Web applications that are different from the legacy or conventional software are as follows (Pressman and Lowe 2008).

- Immediacy (time to market is a few days or weeks);
- Context sensitivity (affected by browser, operating system, server, storage, etc.);
- Content sensitivity (quality and aesthetic nature of content remain important);
- Continuous evolution (unlike planned and time-spaced releases);
- Data drivenness (use of hypermedia to present text, graphics, audio, and video);
- Performance (expectation of less waiting time for server-side processing, client-side formatting, and display);
- Availability ($24 \times 7 \times 365$ for popular Web applications such as Facebook and banking Web sites);
- Aesthetics (look and feel);
- Security (over the network);

- Network intensiveness (large pool of diverse clients);
- Concurrency (huge number of users at the same time);
- Unpredictable load (growing magnitude of user by the day).

1.3.2   Web Applications Versus Semantic Web Applications

SWAs are different from Web applications in terms of openness (W3 2017), as in data stored in and retrieved from heterogeneous sources as on BBC Web site and in terms of computational complexity as in dynamic data at management firms (Antoniou 2012). These unique characteristics of SWAs as opposed to software and Web applications call for a quality model (Azuma 2001) exclusively for SWA (Baliyan and Kumar 2013a, b). Further, the motivation to work in the area of SWAs rises from the fact that the Semantic Web technologies have the potential to devise intelligent applications across various domains such as Chevron, Adaptive Blue, and TripIt (Fluit et al. 2006; Sheth 2006), Power Magpie for semantic Web browsing, PowerAqua for open-domain question answering, etc. (D'Aquin et al. 2008). SWAs have machine comprehensible content that leads to improved cognizance of the information contained in them. This enables their use as better search engines and mobile agents, more advanced knowledge management systems, etc. (Antoniou and Harmelen 2004). A typical SWA comprises a search and inference engine, a user interface to query and response, and data set or ontology to drive it (OAI 2016). Figure 1.4 (Baliyan 2015) shows the relations among Web, Semantic Web, Web applications, and Semantic Web applications.

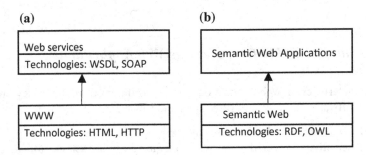

Fig. 1.4   a Relation between Web and Web services; **b** relation between Semantic Web and Semantic Web applications

1.4 Semantic Web Application as a Service

Defining software development from scratch is particularly useful for small- and medium-scale enterprises, start-ups that are numerous in India, while established industry giants will eventually migrate to the cloud. An example of such manifestation is Software as a Service (SaaS) for data-intensive applications such as health care.

For facilitating the software to end user, the usage of SaaS delivery model is rapidly increasing in software industry. The National Institute of Science and Technology (NIST) defines characteristics of cloud computing as:

> On-demand self-service, ubiquitous network access, location independent resource pooling, rapid elasticity, and pay per use. (Spinola 2009)

In SaaS, customers rent software hosted by vendor, e.g., Google Docs. Also called as subscription software, SaaS essentially separates software ownership from the user. The owner is a vendor who hosts the software and lets the user execute it through some form of client-side architecture via Internet or Intranet (Laplante et al. 2008).

Some resultant advantages of SaaS over traditional software are economies of scale, separation of concerns, pay-per-use, on demand, accessibility through Internet, etc. (Pressman and Lowe 2008). SaaS is software delivery model based on the cloud computing and allows customers to rent software hosted by some vendor (Spinola 2009). Quality assessment of Web applications based on SaaS model needs to consider some additional attributes especially due to the reason that SaaS has various characteristics that are different from traditional software delivery models (Baliyan and Kumar 2014a).

SWAs are data intensive and thus can fit well as SaaS on cloud platform. For example, a SWA that stores and retrieves basic health indices such as blood pressure, height, weight may be used in the healthcare domain, and machines can transfer patients' data across hospitals. Such SWA with reusable components has its data backed on the cloud for easy anywhere access. Such Semantic Web-based applications that are neither stand-alone nor merely Web-based, rather available as services to the user in a transparent way, may be called Semantic Web application as a Service (SWAaaS), which tend to cater to the future software (Baliyan and Kumar 2016b).

1.5 Quality

Quality of an object can be defined by its characteristics or attributes. ISO defines software quality as:

> The degree to which the software product satisfies stated and implied needs, when used under specified conditions. (Azuma 2001)

Software quality includes functional quality as well as structural quality. Software functional quality defines the conformance to a given design based on the functional requirements or specifications. It is also termed as the fitness-of-purpose of the software. Structural quality defines the degree to which the software was produced correctly and specifies the conformance to non-functional requirements, which are helpful in delivery of functional requirements (Pressman 2005). Some of the attributes that can be used to assess the software quality are compatibility, correctness, efficiency, flexibility, functionality, integrity, interoperability, maintainability, operability, portability, reliability, usability, and others. To measure software quality, many standards and frameworks have been defined such as ISO 9001/9000-3, the Capability Maturity Model, ANSI/IEEE Std. 730-1989, ESA PSS-05-0 1991 (Jørgensen 1999), McCall's model, Boehm's model, ISO/IEC 9126, ISO/IEC 25010 (Pressman 2005), and others. With respect to software engineering, quality is one of the other several important factors studied by researchers and practitioners (Baliyan and Kumar 2014b; Kundu et al. 2013; Singh et al. 2014) that determines the success or failure of a software product. However, the importance of various quality attributes varies for different stakeholders, different markets, different times, and others.

Like quality assessment of traditional software, the quality assessment of Web applications is one of the important steps in the Web engineering process. However, Web applications may be contrasted with traditional software based on network intensiveness, performance requirements, data-driven nature, continuous evolution, security, aesthetics, and more (Pressman and Lowe 2008). Unlike conventional software that generally has limited number of users at a time, a Web application must allow growing number of users in order to be regarded as of high quality. Some of the important additional quality attributes for Web applications are scalability, presentation, maintenance, ease of use, aesthetics, multimedia richness in contents, communication style, and others. Various models have been defined for formalizing the quality attributes for Web applications such as right weight model (Mich et al. 2003), WQM (Calero et al. 2005), WEF (Zhou 2009), COFUE (De Marsico and Levialdi 2004), and Signore's model (Signore 2005).

Software quality models and metrics have been a part of the software engineering literature since long (Kitchenham and Pfleeger 1996). Similar to the transition that has occurred from stand-alone applications to Web applications, the transition from Web applications to Semantic Web applications is rapidly progressing. Understanding the importance of quality assessment for software applications, the quality assessment of Semantic Web applications is equally needed. SWAs possess some additional characteristics such as machine comprehensibility of the content, sharing and reuse among heterogeneous applications, modular structure of its domain vocabulary, and others. Currently available software quality models do not consider the assessment of these characteristics during software quality evaluation. Hence, they are considered less appropriate or incomplete for assessment of SWAs. A quality model for SWAs has to cater to all layers (see Fig. 1.2), i.e., ontology structure and behavior (Baliyan and Kumar 2016c), overall application and its deployment.

1.6 Conclusion and Summary

Various underlying fundamentals of the book have been presented in this chapter. Basics of Semantic Web, Semantic Web-based applications, ontologies, various quality attributes of Web applications, and Software as a Service are discussed. The chapter also presents motivation for the work and the objectives of this book. In summary,

- SWAs are not just used for information retrieval in a semantic search engine, but are being widely used in the healthcare industry, social networks, e-learning platforms, and multimedia processing.
- Ontology represents knowledge of a particular domain and forms an elementary unit of inference techniques on the Semantic Web. The syntactical composition of ontology as well as its behavior within a Semantic Web-based system or application needs to be assessed.
- For multiple SWAs offering similar functionality, it is imperative to evaluate them and make a choice based on the fulfillment of non-functional requirements by them. The benefits of SWAs can be exploited largely by ensuring their adherence to a clear and validated quality standard.
- SWAs that are neither stand-alone nor merely Web-based, rather available as services to the user in a transparent way, tend to cater to the future software. We focus on providing quality assessment of components of as well as overall SWAs while focusing on their delivery as a service on the cloud.
- There is a need to address the quality assessment of SWAs from bottom to top involving the assessment of underlying ontology, software or application, and deployment as a service, where the ontology designer or user may choose how much and what to assess.

References

Antoniou, G., Van Harmelen, F.: A Semantic Web Primer. MIT press (2004)

Antoniou, G., Corcho, O., Aberer, K., Simperl, E., Studer, R.: Semantic data management (Dagstuhl Seminar 12171). In: Dagstuhl Reports, vol. 2, No. 4. Schloss Dagstuhl-Leibniz-Zentrum fuer Informatik (2012)

Asensio, J.A., Padilla, N., Iribarne, L.: An ontology-driven case study for the knowledge representation of management information systems. In WSKS, pp. 426–432 (2011)

Azuma, M.: SQuaRE: the next generation of the ISO/IEC 9126 and 14598 international standards series on software product quality. European Software Control and Metrics Conference, pp. 337–346 (2001)

Baliyan, N.: Quality assessment of semantic web based applications. Ph.D. Dissertation, Indian Institute of Technology Roorkee (2015)

Baliyan, N., Kumar, S.: Adaptation of software engineering to semantic web based system development. In: 2013 International Conference on Emerging Trends in Communication, Control, Signal Processing and Computing Applications (C2SPCA), pp. 1–5. IEEE (2013a)

Baliyan, N., Kumar, S.: Quality assessment of software as a service on cloud using fuzzy logic. In: 2013 IEEE International Conference on Cloud Computing in Emerging Markets (CCEM), pp. 1–6. IEEE (2013b)

Baliyan, N., Kumar, S.: Towards software engineering paradigm for software as a service. In: 2014 Seventh International Conference on Contemporary Computing (IC3), pp. 329–333. IEEE (2014a)

Baliyan, N., Kumar, S.: Software process and quality evaluation for semantic web applications. IETE Tech. Rev. **31**(6), 452–462 (2014)

Baliyan, N., Kumar, S.: Towards measurement of structural complexity for ontologies. Int. J. Web Eng. Technol. **11**(2), 153–173 (2016a)

Baliyan, N., Kumar, S.: A hierarchical fuzzy system for quality assessment of semantic web application as a service. ACM SIGSOFT Softw. Eng. Notes **41**(1), 1–7 (2016b)

Baliyan, N., Kumar, S.: A behavioral metrics suite for modular ontologies. In: Proceedings of the Second International Conference on Information and Communication Technology for Competitive Strategies, p. 133. ACM (2016c)

Bateman, J., Borgo, S., Lüttich, K., Masolo, C., Mossakowski, T.: Ontological modularity and spatial diversity. Spat. Cogn. Comput. **7**(1), 97–128 (2007)

Berners-Lee, T., Hendler, J., Lassila, O.: The semantic web. Sci. Am. **284**(5), 28–37 (2001)

Blomqvist, E.: The use of semantic web technologies for decision support—a survey. Semant. Web **5**(3), 177–201 (2014)

Briand, L.C., Morasca, S., Basili, V.R.: Property-based software engineering measurement. IEEE Trans. Softw. Eng. **22**(1), 68–86 (1996)

Calero, C., Ruiz, J., Piattini, M.: Classifying web metrics using the web quality model. Online Inf. Rev. **29**(3), 227–248 (2005)

Dalal, S., Kumar, S., Baliyan, N.: An ontology-based approach for test case reuse. In: Intelligent Computing, Communication and Devices, pp. 361–366. Springer, New Delhi (2015)

D'Aquin, M., Motta, E., Sabou, M., et al.: Toward a new generation of semantic web applications., IEEE Intell. Syst. **23**(3), 20–28 (2008)

De Marsico, M., Levialdi, S.: Evaluating web sites: exploiting user's expectations. Int. J. Hum. Comput. Stud. **60**(3), 381–416 (2004)

Ensan, F., Du, W.: A semantic metrics suite for evaluating modular ontologies. Inf. Syst. **38**(5), 745–770 (2013)

Fensel, D. (ed.): Spinning the semantic web: Bringing the World Wide Web to its Full Potential. MIT Press (2005)

Floridi, L.: Web 2.0 vs. the semantic web: a philosophical assessment. Episteme **6**(1), 25–37 (2009)

Fluit, C., Sabou, M., Van Harmelen, F.: Visualizing the Semantic Web, pp. 45–58. Springer, London (2006)

Fugini, M., Teimourikia, M., Hadjichristofi, G.: A web-based cooperative tool for risk management with adaptive security. Future Gener. Comput. Syst. **54**, 409–422 (2016)

Gruber, T.: Ontology. Encyclopedia of Database Systems, pp. 1963–1965 (2009)

Gruber, T.R.: A translation approach to portable ontology specifications. Knowl. Acquis. **5**(2), 199–220 (1993)

Iribarne, L., Padilla, N., Asensio, J.A., Criado, J., Ayala, R., Almendros, J., Menenti, M.: Open-environmental ontology modeling. IEEE Trans. Syst. Man Cybern. Part A Syst. Hum. **41**(4), 730–745 (2011)

Jørgensen, M.: Software quality measurement. Adv. Eng. Softw. **30**(12), 907–912 (1999)

Kitchenham, B., Pfleeger, S.L.: Software quality: the elusive target (special issues section). IEEE Softw. **13**(1), 12–21 (1996)

Kumar, S., Baliyan, N., Sukalikar, S.: Ontology cohesion and coupling metrics. Int. J. Semantic Web Inf. Syst. (IJSWIS) **13**(4), 1–26 (2017)

Kundu, D., Samanta, D., Mall, R.: Automatic code generation from unified modelling language sequence diagrams. IET Softw. **7**(1), 12–28 (2013)

Laplante, P.A., Zhang, J., Voas, J.: What's in a Name? Distinguishing between SaaS and SOA. IT Prof. **10**(3), 46–50 (2008)

McGuinness, D.L., Fikes, R., Hendler, J., Stein, L.A.: DAML + OIL: an ontology language for the semantic web. IEEE Intell. Syst. **17**(5), 72–80 (2002)

Mich, L., Franch, M., Inverardi, P.N., Marzani, P.: Choosing the "rightweight" model for web site quality evaluation. In: International Conference on Web Engineering, pp. 334–337. Springer, Berlin, Heidelberg (2003)

Noy, N.F., Chugh, A., Liu, W., Musen, M.A.: A framework for ontology evolution in collaborative environments. In: International Semantic Web Conference, pp. 544–558. Springer, Berlin, Heidelberg (2006)

OAI: Why evaluating semantic web applications is difficult. http://oai.cwi.nl/oai/asset/12425/12425A.pdf (2016). Accessed 2 October 2016

Pressman, R.S.: Software Engineering: A Practitioner's Approach. Palgrave Macmillan (2005)

Pressman R.S., Lowe D.: Web Engineering: A Practitioner's Approach. McGraw-Hill (2008)

Schwartz, D.G.: From open IS semantics to the semantic web: the road ahead. IEEE Intell. Syst. **18**(3), 52–58 (2003)

Sheth, A. (ed.): Semantic Web-Based Information Systems: State-of-the-Art Applications. IGI Global (2006)

Signore, O.: A comprehensive model for web sites quality. In: Seventh IEEE International Symposium on Web Site Evolution (WSE 2005), pp. 30–36. IEEE (2005)

Singh, L.K., Vinod, G., Tripathi, A.K.: Impact of change in component reliabilities on system reliability estimation. ACM SIGSOFT Softw. Eng. Notes **39**(3), 1–6 (2014)

Smith, P., Prasad, P.W.C., Singh, A.K.,: Cyber schooling: a revolution for the education system. In 2014 2nd International Conference on Emerging Technology Trends in Electronics, Communication and Networking (ET2ECN), pp. 1–5. IEEE (2014)

Spinola, M.: An essential guide to possibilities and risks of cloud computing, p. 2012 (2009). Retrieved 24 Mar 2009

Sukalikar, S., Kumar, S., Baliyan, N.: Analysing cohesion and coupling for modular ontologies. In: 2014 International Conference on Advances in Computing, Communications and Informatics (ICACCI), pp. 2063–2066. IEEE (2014)

Thomasson, A.L.: Ontology made easy. Oxford University Press (2014)

W3: Semantic web use cases and case studies. https://www.w3.org/2001/sw/sweo/public/UseCases/BBC/. Accessed on 25 Jan 2017

Zhou, Z.: Evaluating websites using a practical quality model. Report, De Montfort University (2009)

Chapter 2
Quality Evaluation of Ontologies

Abstract This chapter handles assessment of the innermost layer of the Semantic Web cake, i.e., ontology, through a metrics suite called OntoMod. We assess the syntactical composition of ontology, in addition to its behavioral aspect in a Semantic Web application. Firstly, novel cohesion and coupling metrics have been discussed, which are found to be superior in terms of accuracy and expressive power than existing cohesion and coupling metrics, on sample ontologies. Furthermore, by using continuous scale of measurement, and tackling indirect relationships in ontology, our cohesion and coupling metrics can account for subtle dissimilarities among different modularizations of the same ontology. Hence, a key role of OntoMod is to help the ontology engineer in choosing the most suitable modularization of ontology according to fitness for (re)use, regardless of its type and size. Secondly, improved metrics for structural complexity of an ontology have been formulated. Finally, a few crucial metrics for behavioral assessment of ontology have been adapted from the literature and incorporated in the OntoMod suite. The only precondition for assessing structural and behavioral quality of modular ontology through the OntoMod suite is the availability of partial or complete ontology visualization. This chapter validates each of the constituent OntoMod metrics, either practically on real-world ontologies or theoretically through benchmark validation frameworks.

Keywords Modular ontology · Structural quality · Cohesion · Coupling
Complexity · Behavioral quality

Section 2.1 familiarizes readers with the idea of quality evaluation of modular ontology and the definition of class and property. Section 2.2 gives the related literature's overview. Section 2.3 describes in detail our quality model, called OntoMod. Next, Sect. 2.4 analytically validates the definitions of cohesion, coupling, complexity, and behavioral metrics through standards such as IEEE 1061, Kitchenham's, Briand's, and Weyuker's criteria. Additionally, this section performs comparative evaluation of OntoMod with some existing works. Section 2.5 demonstrates an example computation of OntoMod's quality value through the implementation of a Web application created for this purpose. Lastly, the concluding comments and potential research directions are summarized in Sect. 2.6.

© The Author(s) 2018   19
S. Kumar and N. Baliyan, *Semantic Web-Based Systems*, SpringerBriefs in Computer Science, https://doi.org/10.1007/978-981-10-7700-5_2

2.1   Quality Evaluation of Modular Ontology

Ontology is domain-specific vocabulary expressed as .owl or .rdf file. Its visualization is a graph. The Web of data incorporates explicit semantics/annotates metadata in the form of ontologies, so the data becomes machine-understandable.

The ontology designer increasingly requires relative assessment of and subsequent selection from several semantically equivalent modular ontologies, since it determines how fast the Semantic Web application (SWA) backed by the ontology responds. This selection is often based on verifying the ontology's compliance with a standard quality model. Furthermore, the benefits of SWAs may be exploited to a larger extent by confirming their compliance with a quality metrics suite. Hence, for leveraging the advantages of interoperability, reuse and therefore higher productivity in SWAs, one should screen and improvise the quality of modular ontologies.

To the end of comprehensive evaluation of the modular ontology, this chapter is dedicated to defining a metrics suite (henceforth referred to as OntoMod), for its structural as well as behavioral quality. For formulating OntoMod metrics, the ontology modules have been represented using graph theoretical approach (see Sect. 1.2.1). The objective of this chapter is to define and validate a metrics suite for quality assessment of modular ontology and to illustrate the computations of metric values through a prototype.

Prior to describing OntoMod, it is noted that in RDF schema, a class (or concept) is a resource with rdf: type property having value rdfs: Class of the RDF schema vocabulary. Moreover, a sub-class is defined with the help of rdfs: subClassOf property which follows transitivity in RDF schema. Consider two sets, namely, class and datatype; then, a mapping or relation from an entity in class set to an entity in datatype set is known as data or concrete property. It is declared using the owl: DatatypeProperty constructor. On the other hand, a relation from one class type entity to another class type entity is called object or abstract property. It is declared using the owl: ObjectProperty constructor (Breitman et al. 2007).

2.2   Overview of Some Works on Quality Evaluation of Modular Ontology

A few earlier attempts at quality assessment of modular ontologies are discussed with respect to methodology, tools, contributions, and limitations in Table 2.1.

Baliyan and Kumar (2014) critically review some related works for ontology metrics, as discussed below.

Kang et al. (2004) measured the structural complexity of ontology using weighted class dependence graphs, entropy distance, and static UML diagrams.

In Yao et al.'s work (2005), cardinality (number) of root and external classes, and average depth of hierarchical structure determine ontology's design complexity.

Table 2.1 Summary of works on quality assessment of modular ontology

Reference	Contribution	Methodology	Toolset	Drawback
Zhu et al. (2017)	Objective measurement of ontology quality in the context of semantic description of Web services	Case study on five real-life Web services	In-house tool that implements the metrics	Metrics need time to become mature and is widely accepted
Khan (2016)	Provision of specialized metrics for locality-based modules and partitioning modules	Mathematical equations to assess module quality	Tool for ontology module metrics (TOMM), Protégé	Metrics only pertain to structural aspects of ontology module
Verma (2016)	Selection of appropriate ontology for reuse	Survey and analysis	Abstract framework	No experimentation has been carried out
Hlomani and Stacey (2014)	Comparison of approaches for ontology evaluation	Empirical analysis and extensive survey	Analysis based on various factors	No formulation for new metrics
Duque-Ramos et al. (2013)	Selection of ontology for (re)use by developers	Ontology experts' knowledge	In-house software tool	The tool has not been tested on large-scale ontologies
Ensan and Du (2013)	Assessment of suitability of an ontology in an enterprise domain	Empirical investigation of case studies	Neon toolkit, description logic, conjunctive queries	Precise relation among cohesion, coupling, and design criteria needs exploration
Zhang et al. (2010)	Measurement of design complexity	Weyuker's evaluation criteria for analytical validation	Swoogle ontologies for experimental validation	Relationship between complexity and quality of ontology needs to be investigated
García et al. (2010a)	Coupling metrics for inter-class relationships	Their theory is proven by case study	Validation using public ontology	Class object or class datatype mapping may be captured by new metrics
García et al. (2010b)	Semantic coupling metrics presented	State-of-the-art review and visual analytics	Framework written in Java and Jena API	Semantic coupling metrics not complete

(continued)

Table 2.1 (continued)

Reference	Contribution	Methodology	Toolset	Drawback
Ma et al. (2010)	Cohesion metrics to test inconsistency	Theoretical and experimental validation	Standard test set of debugging ontologies	Metrics are not complete rather complementary to existing cohesion metrics
Evermann and Fang (2010)	Quality of ontology is assessed in terms of its deviation from perceived reality	Principles of cognitive psychology, knowledge representation	SUMO, BWW, and WordNet	Cognitive quality should not independently measure quality
Stvilia (2007)	Quality evaluation of ontology	Development of twelve dimensions and metrics for ontology	Structural and semantic features	Missing analytical and experimental validation
Tartir and Arpinar (2007)	Decision making with the help of custom-tailored quality criteria	Mathematical formulation of schema and instance metrics	Sesame and RDF repository, Swoogle	Ranks only populated ontologies
Yang et al. (2006)	Measurement of complexity of ontology	Concept hierarchy, quantity, ratio, and correlativity of relationships	Metrics suite based on various attributes of concepts	Domain-specific. No analytical validation
Alani et al. (2006)	Ranking of ontologies for use by knowledge engineers	Ranking ontologies based on four measures	Structural features of ontology	Manual intervention and continuous. updation of parameters are required
Orme et al. (2006)	Measurement of coupling in ontology	Cardinality of external class interfaces	External interfaces	Dependency relations of various kinds unaccounted for
Yao et al. (2005)	Measurement of cohesion in ontology	Root and leaf class cardinality	Structural features of ontology	Hierarchical relations in ontology unaccounted for
Kang et al. (2004)	Structural complexity analysis	Weighted class dependence graphs, entropy distance	Unified Modeling Language (UML) diagrams	UML diagrams are static; hence, only static knowledge of ontologies is taken

Orme et al. (2006) formulated an ontology coupling measure by retrieving the count of external classes required to define classes and roles of the ontology, the overall number of leaf class references, and ontology relationships.

Alani et al. (2006) evaluate and grade ontology for appropriateness of reuse, with the help of using four measures as per the requirements of a knowledge engineer.

Yang et al. (2006) measure ontology complexity on the basis of concept hierarchy, and the quantity, ratio, and correlativity of classes and links.

Tartir and Arpinar's (2007) OntoQA permits users to accommodate the ranking concerning some aspects of ontologies, in order to meet their applications' demand. The OntoQA ranking is similar to that of domain experts' ranking.

Stvilia's model (2007) in the context of ontology's intended use has twelve dimensions and metrics for ontology evaluation such as validity, cohesiveness, complexity, semantic consistency, structural consistency. The work uses Morphbank biodiversity research data repository.

Evermann and Fang (2010) focus on assessing the ontology mapping to the domain's implicit conceptual modeling. Their experiments could not find any ontology as having good cognitive quality; however, those ontologies may be regarded as superior quality from the perspective of structure, fitness-of-purpose, functionality, and tool support.

Some cohesion metrics are defined by Ma et al. (2010), i.e., cardinality of ontology partitions, cardinality of minimally inconsistent subsets, and mean value of axiom inconsistencies. They identify inconsistencies, if any, owing to the varying nature of Web and hence measure ontological semantics as opposed to ontological structure.

Analogous to software engineering metrics for coupling, García et al. (2010a) define inter-entity coupling to capture the link between ontologies. Self-coupling occurs when entity fits in both datatype and property value of the same concept.

Appropriate measures of coupling could facilitate the depiction of links among classes in ontology (García et al. 2010b). This work emphasized on semantic coupling in addition to structural coupling between classes in ontology.

Motivated by software metrics for design complexity, Zhang et al. (2010) suggested a similar metric at ontology level and class level. They evaluate the complexity metrics with the help of Weyuker's properties as well as through Swoogle ontologies. Finin et al. (2004) deduce that design complexity deters maintenance and reuse of ontology, thereby degrading its quality.

Ensan and Du (2013) offer cohesion and coupling metrics, by exploiting both tacit and stated knowledge in ontology. A cohesive and loosely coupled ontology is regarded as flexible and shows better reasoning performance.

The ontology quality evaluation framework, OQUARE, has been critiqued by Duque-Ramos et al. (2013); it can assist developers in choosing ontologies for use and reuse. OQUARE uses ontology experts' knowledge for evaluation purpose.

Hlomani and Stacey (2014) underline ontology evaluation based on two aspects, i.e., quality and correctness. Their work analyzes the existent literature in ontology evaluation, metrics, and measures. Their major focus is on data-driven ontology evaluation.

Verma (2016) has surveyed existing works on ontology module metrics and after adding a few more metrics, defined an abstract framework for this purpose. There is a lack of mathematical foundation and experimentation in his submission.

Khan (2016) has attempted to devise specialized measures of modular ontology's quality, additionally; he has developed a tool for the same. However, the metrics continue to address the structural features of ontology, rather than its behavior or semantics.

Zhu et al. (2017) present a unique perspective to ontology assessment by evaluating their quality for Semantic Web service description. The metrics are well defined for such qualitative attributes, and tool for the measurement has been developed. Nevertheless, the applicability and validity of authors' metrics need to be backed by usage or expert's opinion.

The study of the available literature reveals that there is paucity of research in this field; furthermore, in certain works, the parameter selection for some complexity metrics is left to user's discretion (Alani et al. 2006). Moreover, the parameters for existing complexity metrics are defined at schema and instance levels (Tartir and Arpinar 2007; Tartir et al. 2005). Hence, it is imperative to define complexity metrics at a finer granularity within ontology, regardless of it being populated with instances or not. The traditional definition of software quality (Pressman 2005) is not suitably applicable to ontology; therefore, the adaptation of software quality metrics for ontology is presented by Baliyan and Kumar (2014).

Most works available on ontology evaluation either target monolithic ontologies or define metrics for modular ontologies, which are majorly syntax-based or obtained from the graphical depiction of the ontology (Orme et al. 2006; Ma et al. 2010; Oh et al. 2011). As defined in Sect. 1.2.1, modular ontology may have numerous partitions or modules identified by high cohesion among classes belonging to a module and low coupling among classes from different modules (Bateman et al. 2007). There is scarcity of work for computing structural complexity of ontology in the context of relationships between concepts. Although explicitly defined relationships are sometimes handled, they are not categorized on the basis of their comparative effect on ontology (Vrandecic and Sure 2007). Additionally, the effect of relationships which are neither strong nor moderate is yet to be analyzed (Ensan and Du 2013). The assessment of syntactical composition of a modular ontology and, additionally, behavior within SWA remains an open issue.

2.3   A Quality Evaluation Model for Modular Ontology

The OntoMod metrics suite evaluates the quality of modular ontology from two perspectives, namely structural and behavioral. The structural quality is measured directly or indirectly from the ontology visualization in ontology editors. The quality is evaluated by OntoMod, immaterial of the type and dimension of ontology. Cohesion and coupling metrics for modular ontology have been defined in Sect. 2.3.1. Improved attributes and their corresponding metrics for structural complexity of modular ontology have been defined in Sect. 2.3.2. Further, Sect. 2.3.3 compiles some crucial metrics which determine the dynamic behavior of a modular ontology.

2.3.1 Cohesion and Coupling Metrics

The focus of ontology designer is to choose the modular ontology with most suitable trade-off at high intra-modular cohesion and low inter-modular coupling values and subsequently choose the most consistent ontology. Following are the steps to compute cohesion and coupling values in OntoMod, for a particular modular ontology (Kumar et al. 2017).

Input: set S of ontologies

Output: Cohesion and coupling values and ranking of ontologies in S

1. Begin
2. Identify relationships for each concept-pair in ontology
3. Compute strength factor

   for each ontology in S do
       i. Identify link type
       ii. Find distance between concepts
       iii. Consider special cases
   end for

4: Calculate cardinality of modules to find normalization factor
5: Calculate normalized cohesion and coupling values using (2.5) and (2.8)
6: Choose ontology with the maximum cohesion and minimum coupling
7: End

As soon as the modular ontology is fed as input, the cognition of relationships starts. A relationship may encompass multiple concepts. Cautious examination of the relationship structure is necessary to understand the nature of dependency and strength factor (sf) between each pair of concepts. The sf value depends on interpretation of relationship types, distance factor, and consideration of exceptional cases. Then, we compute normalization factors with the help of the cardinality of the module and ontology. Next, the normalized values of cohesion and coupling are computed through the OntoMod metrics. They are subsequently compared for different modularizations of an ontology or different semantically equivalent ontologies, and the user may select the most suitable combination from available modularizations or the most suitable ontology, respectively (Kumar et al. 2017).

Apart from direct links between neighboring concepts, the indirect links between far away concepts also affect cohesion and coupling. The strength factor (sf) of a relationship (link) indicates the dependence that the concepts have on each other.

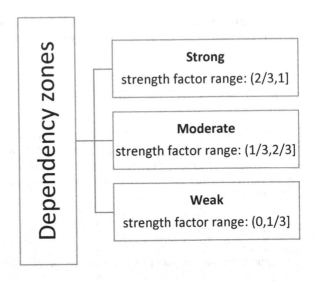

Fig. 2.1 Three dependency zones ($0 \leq$ strength factor ≤ 1)

The sf depends on the type of relationship and on the distance between concepts. We present sf that can vary continuously in the range (0,1], which is further distributed into three zones, namely strong, moderate, and weak as seen in Fig. 2.1.

The links that have a great effect on cohesion and coupling fall in strong zone, with sf ranging in (2/3, 1]. The links which moderately affect cohesion and coupling correspond to sf in the range (1/3, 2/3], i.e., the moderate zone. A few ontology links are particularly uncertain and thus have a weak impact on cohesion and coupling. Such links fall in the weak dependency zone with sf in (0, 1/3] (Kumar et al. 2017).

In the past, Ensan and Du (2013) have applied formalism to categorize inter-concept links as strong or moderate. In addition, discrete weights are assigned to reflect the links' intensities. They experimentally validated the ratio of sf for 'strong link' to sf for 'moderate link' to be 2:1 (Ensan and Du 2013). As an intuitive extension, the proportion of upper limits of the sf of strong, moderate, and weak link is fixed at 3:2:1. Let us now define some terminology that forms background of our cohesion and coupling metrics.

> A concept is said to be dependent on the other if the former's constraints and properties are determined either fully or partially by the latter's semantics.

> A strong dependency exists between two concepts if the interpretation of the former is incomplete without the interpretation of latter.

Fig. 2.2 Visualization of
$X \cap Y$

One may draw an analogy between total participation in an Extended Entity-Relationship diagram and strong dependency in ontology. Similarly, in the Attribute Language with Complement, a strong dependency is analogous to strict class to class binding via object property or strict class to datatype binding via data property. Formally speaking, the value restriction $\forall L.C$ fires if a strong dependency occurs; i.e., if $C_1 \sqsubseteq \forall L.C_2$, then C_1 and C_2 have strong dependency and $C_1 \sqsubseteq C_2$ (Kumar et al. 2017).

Let **X** be a set of fathers and **Y** be a set of men. A father is mandatorily a man, hence $\mathbf{X} \sqsubseteq \mathbf{Y}$; here **X** is strongly dependent on **Y**. In addition, let **L** be a link called **hasChild**. Every man who has a child will be a father; i.e., every element of set **Y** with link **L** will be an element of set **X**, i.e., $\mathbf{X} \sqsubseteq \forall L.\mathbf{Y}$. In this case also, **X** is strongly dependent on **Y**. Figure 2.2 shows $\mathbf{X} \cap \mathbf{Y}$ in Randolph diagram where / is for X and \ is for Y. Barksdale (2018), assuming countably infinite sets. Figure 2.2 represents strong dependency when the dot is equivalent to the set X.

A weak dependency exists between two concepts if the interpretation of the first is dependent on the second, subject to some constraints specified by other concepts.

Let $\mathbf{X}_1 \cap \mathbf{X}_2 \sqsubseteq \mathbf{Y}$, where $\mathbf{X}_1, \mathbf{X}_2$ and **Y** are ontology concepts. If $\mathbf{X}_2$ tends to universal set, i.e., $\mathbf{X}_2 \rightarrow \mathbf{U}$, then $\mathbf{X}_1 \cap \mathbf{X}_2 \rightarrow \mathbf{X}_1$ and $\mathbf{X}_1 \sqsubseteq \mathbf{Y}$. Hence, $\mathbf{X}_1$ has strong dependency on **Y** and weak dependency on $\mathbf{X}_2$. Let $\mathbf{X}_1$ be a set of college students, $\mathbf{X}_2$ be a set of students with sports grant, and **Y** be a set of college students who play sports. Here, $\mathbf{X}_1$, $\mathbf{X}_2$, and **Y** are almost independent of each other. When every college student has sports grant ($\mathbf{X}_2 \rightarrow \mathbf{U}$), then $\mathbf{X}_1$ will be contained in **Y**. Whereas when no student plays sports ($\mathbf{Y} \rightarrow \mathbf{\Phi}$), then $\mathbf{X}_1 \cap \mathbf{X}_2 = \mathbf{\Phi}$ and a strong link $\mathbf{X}_1 \sqsubseteq \mathbf{X}_2$ exists. Here, $\mathbf{X}_1$ and $\mathbf{X}_2$ have weak and strong dependencies on **Y**, respectively.

In other words, a weak dependency is manifested as the constraint $\exists L.\mathbf{X} \sqsubseteq \mathbf{Y}$; i.e., just the elements of **X** which are a part of the link **L** form a subset of **Y**. Here, the set **X** may be interpreted even without **Y**. Figure 2.2 shows weak dependency where there are some elements in $\mathbf{X} \cap \mathbf{Y}$.

Fig. 2.3 Visualization of
$Y_1 \cup Y_2$

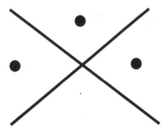

> A moderate dependency exists between two concepts if the dependency is neither strong nor weak.

Figure 2.3 shows $Y_1 \cup Y_2$ for moderate dependency in Randolph diagram, assuming countably infinite sets where / is for Y_1 and \ is for Y_2 (Barksdale 2018). For $X \sqsubseteq Y_1 \cup Y_2$, one of the three cases may arise, i.e., $X \cong Y_1 \cup Y_2$, $Y_1 \cup Y_2 \rightarrow Y_2$ (or $X \sqsubseteq Y_2$), $Y_1 \cup Y_2 \rightarrow Y_1$ (or $X \sqsubseteq Y_1$).

For direct links, the sf is obtained based on the dependency zone. Further, $0 < sf \leq 1$ and $sf \in R^+$. The sf is inversely related to the distance d between the concepts (Oh et al. 2011), i.e., $sf \propto 1/d$. For indirect links involving numerous indirect links, the sf can be obtained from (2.1) as:

$$sf = 1/((1/sf_1) + (1/sf_2) + \cdots + sf_i \cdots + (1/sf_n)) \qquad (2.1)$$

where sf_i is sf of intermediary links in an indirect relationship, s.t. $1 \leq i < n$ and $i \in Z^+$ where n is the number of concepts.

It should be noted that for $n = 1$, $sf = 1/(1/sf_1)$ and for $n \rightarrow \infty$, $sf \rightarrow \Phi$. This is because with an increasing number of links, the distance and impact of dependency decrease, and thus sf decreases. This helps us to deal with extremely huge ontology.

Besides direct and indirect links between a pair of concepts at a time, multiple concepts may be involved in direct links. In such cases, the dependencies become more complex (Ensan and Du 2013). Kumar et al. (2017) define a few such scenarios below.

Case 1: $A \sqsubseteq B_1 \cup B_2 \cup \ldots B_i \ldots \cup B_n$, *where* $2 \leq n < \infty$ *and* $n \in Z^+$

From discussion on Fig. 2.3, it follows that A moderately depends on B_i. With a change in n value, the sf value changes in the moderate range, viz., $(1/3, 2/3]$. For $A \sqsubseteq B_1 \cup B_2$, $n = 2$, sf tends to the upper bound of the moderate interval, i.e., $2/3$. With an increasing n value, the likelihood of A being a part of any B_i slowly reduces, and consequently, the dependency of A on any B_i also reduces. As $n = \infty$, sf tends to the lower bound of the moderate interval, i.e., $1/3$. The sf for Case 1 may be formulated in (2.2) below.

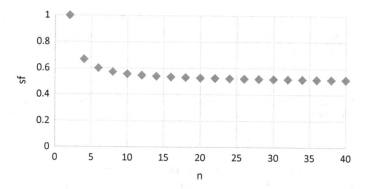

Fig. 2.4 *n* versus sf for Case 1

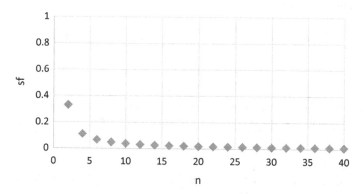

Fig. 2.5 *n* versus sf for Case 2

$$sf_{AB_i} = \frac{1}{3} \times \left(1 + \left(\frac{1}{n-1}\right)\right) \qquad (2.2)$$

Figure 2.4 visualizes the effect of *n* on sf_{AB_i} for Case 1.

Case 2: $A_1 \cap A_2 \cap \ldots A_i \ldots \cap A_N \sqsubseteq B$, *where* $2 \leq n < \infty$ *and* $n \in Z^+$

From discussion on Fig. 2.2, it follows that A_k weakly depends on A_i and B, where $i \in [1, n] - \{k\}$; yet, with a change in n value, the sf value changes in moderate range, viz., (0,1/3). For $A_1 \cap A_2 \sqsubseteq B$, $n = 2$, sf tends to the top threshold of weak range, i.e., 1/3. With an increasing *n* value, the chance of A_k to depend on either A_i or B continues to decrease, where $i \in [1, n] - \{k\}$. As $n \to \infty$, sf tends to the lower limit of weak interval, i.e., 0. The sf for Case 2 may be formulated in (2.3) below.

$$sf_{A_k B} \quad \text{or,} \quad sf_{A_k A_i} = \frac{1}{3} \times \left(\frac{1}{n-1}\right) \quad \text{where,} \quad 2 \leq n < \infty, \quad n \in Z^+ \qquad (2.3)$$

Figure 2.5 visualizes the effect of *n* on $sf_{A_k B}$ or $sf_{A_k A_i}$ for Case 2.

Case 3: $A \sqsubseteq B_1 \cap B_2 \cap \ldots B_i \ldots \cap B_N$, *where* $2 \leq n < \infty$ *and* $n \in Z^+$

A is strongly dependent on B_i, where $i \in [1, n]$. In a situation like this, even if n increases, A will be included in all B_i values. Hence, this link is independent of the cardinality of concepts.

If ontology O be composed of n modules $m_1, m_2 \ldots m_n$, the module cardinality is defined as the number of concepts contained in it, and is denoted by $|m_i|$, where $i \in [1, n]$.

The cohesion of a module m_i is directly proportional to the combined sf of intra-modular dependencies (between all concept pairs considered one by one). In the case of independent concepts, the sf is 0. Thus, the following relation holds (Ensan and Du 2013; Oh et al. 2011).

$$\text{Cohesion}(m_i) \propto \sum C_k \in m_i \sum c_j \in m_i \left(sf\left(c_k, c_j\right) \right) \tag{2.4}$$

For a module m, the normalized value of cohesion is the module cohesion per link. It is denoted by Cohesion $N(m)$.

Oh et al. (2011) set $|m|(|m| - 1)/2$ as the normalization factor. It denotes the highest possible number of intra-modular links that with highest sf will give highest value of total sf in a module. Therefore,

$$\text{Cohesion } N(m_i) = 2/|m_i|(|m_i| - 1) \times \sum c_k \in m_i \sum c_j \in m_i \left(sf\left(c_k, c_j\right) \right) \tag{2.5}$$

As a general rule, for any module m, cohesion may be defined by (2.6) (Kumar et al. 2017) as:

$$\text{Cohesion } (m) = 2/|m|(|m| - 1) \times \sum c_k \in m \sum c_j \in m \left(sf_{\left(c_k, c_j\right)} \right) \tag{2.6}$$

The cardinality of an ontology o is defined as the total number of concepts existing in an ontology and is denoted by $|o|$.

The cohesion of a module m_i is directly proportional to the combined sf of inter-modular dependencies (between all inside–outside concept pairs taken one at a time). In the case of independent concepts, the sf is 0. Thus, for ontology o, the following relation holds (Ensan and Du 2013; Oh et al. 2011).

$$\text{Coupling}\ (m) \propto \sum c_k \in m \sum c_j \in (o - m_i)\left(\text{sf}_{(c_k, c_j)}\right) \qquad (2.7)$$

For a module m, the normalized value of coupling is defined as the module coupling per link. It is denoted by Coupling $N(m)$.

Ensan and Du (2013) set $|m| \times (|o| - |m|)$ as the normalization factor. It indicates the maximum count of inter-modular links. Considering these many relations, each with maximum sf will give a maximum limit of total sf in a module. This is the standard against which the ratio may be calculated for each module. Hence, as per Kumar et al. (2017),

$$\text{Coupling}\ N(m) = 1/|m||o - m| \times \left(\sum c_k \in m \sum c_j \in (o - m_i)\left(sf_{(c_k, c_{yj})}\right)\right) \tag{2.8}$$

2.3.2   Complexity Metrics

In order to handle large-sized ontologies, an understanding of the complexity of ontology could be useful. It is likely that lower the complexity, better is the quality of ontology. Baliyan and Kumar's (2016a) ontology complexity evaluation metrics suite, called ComplexOnto, assesses complexity at various levels of perception. ComplexOnto score shows a positive correlation with the popularity of ontology. Since ontology has characteristics of coherence and reusability, ComplexOnto metrics are inspired from software metrics (Pressman 2005) and component-based software engineering (CBSE) metrics (Narasimhan and Hendradjaya 2007). Following are the steps to compute complexity of a modular ontology using ComplexOnto (Baliyan and Kumar 2016a).

Input: Set S = {RDF/OWL files obtained from semantic search engine}

Output: ComplexOnto score and ranking of ontologies in S
1: Begin
2: for each ontology in S do

    i.   input ontology to ontology editor
   ii.   calculate LD, LC, LR, and CC using (2.9)–(2.12).
  iii.   calculate ComplexOnto score using (2.13)
      end for

3:   contrast ComplexOnto scores for ontologies in S.

4:   select ontology with minimum score
5:   end

Baliyan and Kumar (2016a) list the of ComplexOnto metrics.

- N Count of classes
- $_2^nC$ Maximum count of possible links
- op   Count of object properties
- dp   Count of data properties
- l op + dp , i.e., number of non-subclass links
- sc   Count of sub-class axioms
- LD   Link density
- LC   Links per concept
- LR   Link richness
- CC   Cyclomatic complexity
- w_1 to w_4 Weights assigned to LD, LC, LR, and CC

Each ComplexOnto metric assesses the ontology's ability for knowledge representation at a particular level of abstraction. ComplexOnto uses independent variables in the ontology graph structure that build on ontology artifacts whose values may be computed through ontology editors.

"Link density is the ratio of number of non-subclass links to the maximum possible number of links in an ontology" (Baliyan and Kumar 2016a).

Link density is computed at the highest level of abstraction and is analogous to Component Interaction Density (CID) metrics of CBSE since ontology links are analogous to component interactions. However, since ontology links are symmetric, i.e., equally affect all involved concepts, they are considered undirected. Therefore, (Baliyan and Kumar 2016a) do not define separate metrics for ontology incoming and outgoing interaction density. The link density metric is defined by (2.9) (Baliyan and Kumar 2016a) as:

$$LD = (op + dp)/_2^nC \qquad (2.9)$$

The LD metric is meant to be used at the time of ontology design to show the utilization of links in a given ontology. In an ontology with high LD, concepts independently represent an entity and also the links render the ontology highly complex. In Fig. 2.6, op = 4, dp = 1, $n = 4$, from (2.9), $LD = (4 + 1)/_2^4C$, LD = 0.833.

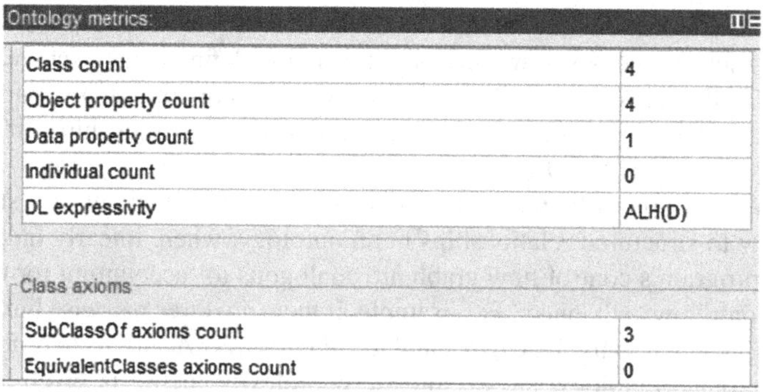

Ontology metrics:	⬚⊟
Class count	4
Object property count	4
Data property count	1
Individual count	0
DL expressivity	ALH(D)
Class axioms	
SubClassOf axioms count	3
EquivalentClasses axioms count	0

Fig. 2.6 Example ontology metrics in (Baliyan and Kumar 2016a)

> Links per concept is the ratio of total number of links to the number of concepts (Baliyan and Kumar 2016a).

This metric points to the spread of links across concepts; these links can be attributed to object properties or data properties (Breitman et al. 2007). It is defined by (2.10) (Baliyan and Kumar 2016a) as:

$$LC = (op + dp)/n \qquad (2.10)$$

Links are non-trivial relationships between concepts in an ontology, so it is crucial to measure the average number of links per concept to capture the knowledge of a domain. McCabe proved that with every additional decision node (one with multiple outgoing edges) the program complexity increases (McCabe 1976). Analogously, with every additional concept with multiple links, the ontology complexity increases. In Fig. 2.6, from (2.10), $LC = (4 + 1)/4$, $LC = 1.25$.

> Link richness is defined as the ratio of non-subclass links to the total number of links (Baliyan and Kumar 2016a).

The link richness metric derives from relationship richness metrics defined by Tartir and Arpinar (2007) which is the number of relationships being used by class instances divided by the number of relationships defined for that class at schema level. Hence, the metric is defined by (2.11) (Baliyan and Kumar 2016a) as:

$$LR = (op + dp)/(op + dp + sc) \qquad (2.11)$$

Link richness gives an insight into the utilization of relationships at the instance level. This metric specifies how well the information defined at the schema level is extracted (Tartir and Arpinar 2007). LR can assist in comparing two ontologies that have similar schemas and yet utilize different number of relationships. In Fig. 2.6, sc = 3, from (2.11), LR = 0.625.

Baliyan and Kumar (2016a) extend McCabe's (1976) argument of a structured control flow to structured relationships in an ontology, where linearly independent paths in a program's control flow graph are analogous to 'accounting for transitive links in an ontology, only once.' For example, if there are three pairwise links among concepts A, B, and C, namely AB, BC, and AC, then merely AC needs to be identified. Therefore, for an ontology, the cyclomatic complexity metric is given by (2.12) (Baliyan and Kumar 2016a) as:

$$CC = (op + dp + sc) - n + 2 \qquad (2.12)$$

We assume that the complete ontology is a connected component, analogous to the definition of McCabe's cyclomatic complexity for a module's graph. The transitive links in ontology signify that two concepts are related via direct link as well as via indirect links. Such transitive links produce cycles in the ontology visualization. Hence, cyclomatic complexity determines the number of linearly independent paths in an ontology. Large number of paths generally indicate unique links in ontology, which renders it more complex. In Fig. 2.6, from (2.12), CC = 6.

Now that we have defined the four complexity metrics; let us look at the computation of ComplexOnto score. We assume that the ontologies are either made accessible to the user or obtained through a keyword-based search on a semantic search engine. Next, an ontology editor is used for semi-automated computation of ComplexOnto score. Since the ComplexOnto metrics, namely, LD, LC, LR, and CC cover an increasing amount of information about ontology in that order, the least amount of information is gained from the most abstract metric, i.e., LD, while CC is the most concrete metric. Apart from adding up to unity, the weights assigned to LD, LC, LR, and CC should ideally be decided after numerous experimental runs. As of now, equal weights of 0.25 have been allotted to each component of ComplexOnto score. The total complexity score for ontology can be computed through weighted sum method, as in (2.13) (Baliyan and Kumar 2016a).

$$\text{ComplexOnto score} = \sum_{i=1}^{4} w_i \times \text{metric}_i \qquad (2.13)$$

where metric$\{\} = \{$LD, LC, LR, CC$\}$ and $\sum_{i=1}^{4} w_i = 1$.

2.3.3 Behavioral Metrics

One should evaluate a modular ontology, not merely from the point of view of its structure, rather also from the perspective of its inherent features, which significantly influence its behavior. After careful study of the literature relevant to ontology metrics for knowledge contained in ontology, knowledge encapsulation, relationship and concept coverage, and depth of subsumption hierarchy have been identified. The knowledge contained in an ontology determines its behavior, which then influences the SWA backed by it. We discuss behavior metrics that are unambiguous and applicable to any type of ontology, such as cross-domain, domain, application, or task ontology. Below, we list the steps to compute behavioral metrics in an ontology, provided that the visualization of ontologies or their partitions are accessible to the ontology engineer (Baliyan and Kumar 2016b).

Input: ontology artifacts
Output: behavioral quality metrics
A = {a$_1$, a$_2$, . . . , a$_n$} is the set of ontologies or the set of ontology partitions.
1: Begin
2: For each ontology a in A
   obtain knowEncap, Cov, and DIT from (2.14), (2.17), and (2.18)
   end for
3: Obtain behavioral quality using (2.19)
4: Rank ontologies of A in decreasing order of behavioral quality
5: End

Let us now define each behavioral metric.

Knowledge encapsulation is the provision for ontology modules to hide their detailed knowledge base and axioms and reveal only the necessary sections to other ontology modules (Baliyan and Kumar 2016b).

Knowledge encapsulation pertains to polymorphism in ontologies; i.e., a concept may be defined from multiple points of view (Ensan and Du 2010). Hence, multiple ontology modules may use a concept, while the precise meaning of that concept may be specialized as part of further research work. Knowledge encapsulation, denoted by knowEncap, here is defined in Ensan and Du (2010) as the ratio of the sum of interface concepts and interface roles (or links) to the sum of all concepts and roles in the modules, as in (2.14) (Baliyan and Kumar 2016b).

$$\text{knowEncap} = 1 - \frac{\text{NiC}_{\text{MO}} + Ni\,Roles_{\text{MO}}}{\sum \text{NC}_{\text{MO}} + \sum \text{NRoles}_{\text{MO}}} \qquad (2.14)$$

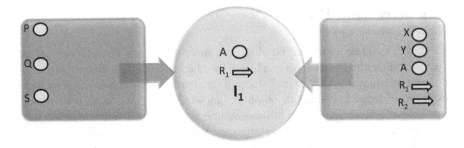

Fig. 2.7 Knowledge encapsulation

where

NiC_{MO}	Count of interface concepts in the modules
$NiRoles_{MO}$	Count of interface roles in the modules
NC_{MO}	Count of concepts in the modules
$NRoles_{MO}$	Count of roles in the modules

In Fig. 2.7,

$$P \sqsubseteq I_1 : A,$$
$$Q \sqsubseteq I_1 : R_1.S,$$
$$NiC_{MO} = 1 (\text{i.e. } A),$$
$$NiRoles_{MO} = 1 (\text{i.e } R_1),$$
$$\sum NC_{MO} = 7 (\text{i.e. } P, Q, S, X, Y, A)$$
$$\sum NRoles_{MO} = 2 (\text{i.e } R_1 \text{ and } R_2)$$

From (2.14), $knowEncap = 1 - \frac{(1+1)}{(6+2)} = 0.75$.

Coverage of ontology affects the range of concepts and relationships covered by ontology (Ouyang et al. 2011). A rich ontology should be sufficiently dense and should have relationships with minimum overlaps. In addition, majority of its search terms should be labeled relationships of concepts (Ouyang et al. 2011).

Concept coverage of ontology indicates its capability to express knowledge about concepts through pertinent relationships among them (Baliyan and Kumar 2016b).

Concept coverage (Con_Cov) is defined in (2.15) (Baliyan and Kumar 2016b).

$$Con\_Cov(O, T) = \frac{\sum_{j=1}^{k} \sum_{i=1}^{n} f(c_i, t_j)}{k} \tag{2.15}$$

where

$C = \{c_1, c_2, \ldots, c_n\}$ is the set of n concepts
$T = \{t_1, t_2, \ldots, t_n\}$ is the set of k search terms for the ontology's domain

$$f(c, t) = \begin{cases} 1, & \text{label}(c) = t \\ 0, & \text{label}(c) \neq t \end{cases}$$

That is, if there is a search term t in one ontology, $f(c, t)$ to 1, else $f(c, t)$ is 0.

> Relationship coverage of ontology reflects its capability to encompass as many diverse relationships as possible (Baliyan and Kumar 2016b).

Relationship coverage (Rel_Cov) is defined in (2.16) (Baliyan and Kumar 2016b).

$$\text{Rel}_{\text{Cov}(O,T)} = 2 \times \frac{\sum_{i=1}^{n} \sum_{j=1, i \neq j}^{n} g(c_i, c_j)}{n(n-1)} \tag{2.16}$$

where

$$g(c_i, c_j) = \begin{cases} 1, & if \text{ there is a relation between } c_i \text{ and } c_j \\ 0, & \text{otherwise} \end{cases}$$

and $\frac{n(n-1)}{2}$ is the number of possible relationships among n concepts.

Ontology coverage is given by (2.17) (Baliyan and Kumar 2016b).

$$\text{Cov}(O) = \alpha \times \text{Con\_Cov}(O) \times \text{Rel\_Cov}(O) \tag{2.17}$$

where α has been fixed through heuristics or using experts' knowledge so that it achieves the best value after numerous experimental trials, and maximizes ontology coverage.

> Depth of subsumption hierarchy is defined as DIT, i.e., the length of the largest path from 'Thing' (top most class) to a leaf class (Baliyan and Kumar 2016b).

This is in analogy with depth of inheritance tree in object-oriented metrics (Duque-Ramos et al. 2011) and is formulated in (2.18) by Baliyan and Kumar (2016b).

$$\text{DIT} = \text{Max}\left(\sum D|c_i|\right) \tag{2.18}$$

where c_i are the leaf classes and $D|c_i|$ is the length of the path from the ith leaf class of the ontology to Thing class.

This metric reflects the richness of ontology with respect to the hierarchical structure composed of concepts. The comprehensive behavioral quality of ontology is obtained as in (2.19), using weighted sum method on the behavioral metrics defined above.

$$\text{Behavioral quality} = w_1 \times \text{knowEncap} + w_2 \times \text{Cov} + w_3 \times \text{DIT} \qquad (2.19)$$

where w_i are weights of corresponding behavioral metrics.

2.4   Validation

Briand et al. (1996) formulated criteria for validating metrics, such as size, coupling, and cohesion irrespective of any software artifact. Briand's framework is unambiguous and thorough as it is grounded on explicitly defined mathematical notions. Thus, it may be applied to validate OntoMod's structural metrics. A metric that adheres to the properties stated in Briand's framework may be established to be properly defined.

Validation of Cohesion, Coupling, and Complexity by Briand's Framework

Baliyan and Kumar (2016a) validate ComplexOnto by Briand's criteria as follows.
  Criterion: Nonnegativity and normalization
  Conformity:

- The cohesion and coupling values are nonnegative and fall in $(0,1]$, so it is normalized for every ontology module.
- In Sect. 2.3.2, op, dp, and $n \in Z^+$, thus LD, LC, and LR are nonnegative. If $n - l \geq 2$ or $l - n < -2$, then the ontology contains very less links as compared to the number of concepts. It is not a probable situation for real ontologies, because the motive of ontology is to indicate links among concepts. If the concepts are unrelated or only slightly related, they may not be contained in a domain ontology. Hence, one may assume that $l - n \leq -2$ and $CC > 0$. From (2.13), ComplexOnto is nonnegative.

  Criterion: Null value
  Conformity:

- In the absence of any intra-modular (inter-modular) links, the cohesion (coupling) metric is null.
- If $l = 0$, then LD, LC, LR, and $CC = 0$; hence from (2.13), ComplexOnto $= 0$.

  Criterion: Symmetry
  Conformity:

- Cohesion is defined for a single module, while coupling between module A and B is same as that between B and A.

- If the direction of a link is reversed, it is renamed accordingly. The links 'State has head Chief Minister' and 'Chief Minister is head of State' both have the same meaning. Here, R: hasHead, Domain: State, Range: Chief Minister, R^{-1}: isHeadOf, Domain: Chief Minister, Range: State. Hence, symmetry is maintained in ComplexOnto metrics.

Criterion: Monotonicity, i.e., if a link is added to a module or between modules, the metric cannot be lesser than what it was before the addition of that link.
Conformity:

- Since there is an additive relation among various links and the values of cohesion and coupling are nonnegative, they do not reduce with the addition of new links to the module(s).
- The complexity of a system is greater than or equal to the sum of the complexities of any two of its modules (say m_1 and m_2) with no links in common.

$$m_1 = \langle n_{m1}, l_{m1} \rangle$$
$$m_2 = \langle n_{m2}, l_{m2} \rangle$$
$$m_1 \cup m_2 \subseteq S$$
$$l_{m1} \cap l_{m2} = \varphi$$
$$\Rightarrow \text{Complexity}(S) \geq \text{Complexity}(m_1) + \text{Complexity}(m_2)$$

Criterion: Merging of modules, i.e., if unconnected modules are merged, the cohesion of the combined module will always be less than or equal to the maximum cohesion of the initial modules.
Conformity:

- Cohesion does not increase after composition of independent modules.

i.e., $\text{Cohesion}(m_{1\cup 2}) = Cohesion(m_1) + Cohesion(m_2) - \text{Cohesion}(m_{1\cap 2})$

Using the first criterion, it is known that Cohesion $(m_{1\cap 2}) \geq 0$.

$$\text{Cohesion } (m_{1\cup 2}) \leq \text{Cohesion}(m_1) + \text{Cohesion}(m_2)$$
$$ormax\{\text{Cohesion}(m_1'), \text{Cohesion}(m_2')\} \geq \text{Cohesion } (m'')$$

- Coupling does not increase after composition of independent modules since the modules may share a few inter-modular links.

i.e., $\text{Coupling}(m_{1\cup 2}) = \text{Coupling}(m_1) + \text{Coupling}(m_2) - \text{Coupling}(m_{1\cap 2})$

Using the first criterion, Coupling $(m_{1\cap 2}) \geq 0$. Thus,

$$\text{Coupling } (m_{1\cup 2}) \leq \text{Coupling}(m_1) + \text{Coupling}(m_2).$$

Criterion: Disjoint module additivity
Conformity:

- If unconnected modules are merged, the coupling of the combined module is equal to the sum of couplings of initial modules.

$$\text{i.e., Coupling } (m_{1\cup2}) = \text{Coupling}(m_1) + \text{Coupling}(m_2) - \text{Coupling}(m_{1\cap2})$$

$\text{Coupling}(m_{1\cap2}) = \emptyset$, because there are no common links between the concepts of m_1 and m_2

$$\text{Coupling } (m_{1\cup2}) = \text{Coupling}(m_1) + Coupling(m_2).$$

- The complexity of a system $S = \langle n, l \rangle$ consisting of disjoint modules, m_1 and m_2, is equal to the sum of the complexities of the two modules.

$$S = \langle n, l \rangle, \quad S = m_1 \cup m_2, \quad m_1 \cap m_2 = \varphi$$
$$\Rightarrow \text{Complexity}(S) = \text{Complexity}(m_1) + \text{Complexity}(m_2)$$

Validation of Behavioral Metrics by IEEE Std 1061

IEEE STD 1061, (1998) provides "a procedure for forming quality requirements and recognizing, applying, examining, and authenticating process and product software quality metrics".

This section validates the application of proposed behavior metrics that rely on the general criteria of IEEE Standard 1061 for software artifacts (IEEE Std 1061, 1998).

Criterion: Correlation. Is there a sufficiently high degree of direct relation between quality attributes and their metrics, to authorize the metric's usage in lieu of the quality attribute, if it is not practical to use the latter.

Conformity: Our metrics have been framed from the definition of factors affecting behavioral quality or adapted from available works. Thus, there exists a high degree of direct relation between quality attributes and their metrics.

Criterion: Tracking. If a metric is directly (or inversely) linked to a quality attribute, for a specific product, then a shift in a quality attribute value shall be coupled with a shift in metric value from the same (or opposite) direction.

Conformity: Each behavioral metric, here, is either directly or indirectly calculable and has positive correlation with quality, by definition, hence traceability.

Criterion: Consistency. Is there consistency between the ranks of quality attributes of a group of software artifact (or ontology) and the ranks of the metric values for that group of software artifact (ontology)? It determines if a metric is able to provide an accurate quality ranking of a set of products or not.

Conformity: If attributes $A_1, A_2, \ldots, A_n$ have a relation $A_1 > A_2 > \cdots > A_n$, then corresponding metrics $M_1, M_2, \ldots, M_n$ have the relation $M_1 > M_2 >$

$\cdots > M_n$. For instance, if relationship coverage $>$ number of interface concepts, then coverage value $>$ knowledge encapsulation, other factors remaining fixed. The metrics are obtained based on the values of determinants of behavioral quality of modular ontology, so consistency is evident from these metrics.

Criterion: Discriminative Power. Does the metric distinguish between high-quality and low-quality software artifacts? The set of metric values concerned with former should be considerably more than those concerned with the latter. It assists in fixing the boundaries of metric values for filtering software artifacts with unacceptable quality.

Conformity: The metric distinguishes between high-and low-quality ontology. Consider three modular ontologies with ranking ontology$_x$ < ontology$_z$ < ontology$_y$, for all attributes in modular ontology's behavioral quality, the quality of ontology would rank as ontology$_x$ < ontology$_z$ < ontology$_y$, given that structural quality (cohesion, coupling, and complexity) remains fixed.

Comparative Analysis

In this section, some prominent works on measurement of cohesion and coupling of ontology are summarized.

Yao et al. (2005) do not provide discussion on coupling and a variety of relationship types in ontology hierarchy. Whereas, the work of Orme et al. (2006) discusses coupling measurement, and not cohesion measurement. Ma et al. (2010) suggest a semantic instead of syntactic suite of cohesion metrics, which depends on the cardinality of ontology partitions, of minimal inconsistent subsets, and average value of axiomatic inconsistencies. These metrics keep the ontological structure unchanged.

Oh et al. (2011) do not account for various types of relationships and their impact on cohesion and coupling values, assigning equal weights to all of them. Although the negative correlation of strength with distance in indirect relations is taken care of, it is computed while ignoring the type of relationship.

Ensan and Du (2013) define a metrics suite for cohesion and coupling in monolithic and modular ontologies, using semantic definitions to differentiate relationships as strong and not-strong (moderate) . However, their metric does not handle diminishing strength of relationship with increasing distance among concepts. In addition, the values for strong and moderate relationship types do not spread over a range to encompass individual strengths across relationships.

To sum up, the current metrics for ontology cohesion and coupling are majorly syntax-based and obtained from ontology visualization. Moreover, the relationships are not distinguished according to their comparative effect on the ontology; rather, only well-defined relationships are accounted for (Vrandečić and Sure 2007). In this direction, Sukalikar et al. (2014) offer to support the ontology engineer in finding the most suitable modularization as per quality, keeping in mind the ontology relationships' type and strength.

Table 2.2 (Kumar et al. 2017) showcases a comparative analysis of the OntoMod model with related works, from the perspective of their salient features. Previously, authors only partially handled hierarchical ontology's relationships (Ensan and Du 2013), (Oh et al. 2011), and (Abbès et al. 2012). It is believed that the mathematical

Table 2.2 Comparative evaluation of cohesion and coupling metrics

Feature	Work			
	OntoMod	Oh et al. (2011)	Abbes et al. (2012)	Ensan and Du (2013)
Ontology visualization	✓	✓	✓	✓
Continuous range of dependency strength	✓	✗	✗	✗
Variable dependency for concepts in conjunction	✓	✗	✗	✗
Consideration to various types of relationships	✓	Hierarchical and non-hierarchical	Hierarchical and non-hierarchical	✓

formulations of cohesion and coupling by Kumar et al. (2017) contribute productively to a sound conceptual basis for their measurement in partial ontologies whose view is hidden from ontology designers. It is not claimed that the OntoMod measures are superior; rather, they are relevant for modular ontologies whose partitions' size may be managed by an average user. These measures of coupling and cohesion are generic since they are applicable to all types of ontology (Kumar et al. 2017).

Very few papers are directed toward evaluating ontology complexity. AKTiveR-ank leaves the choice of parameters for assessing certain complexity metrics at the discernment of user (Alani et al. 2006), while, in ComplexOnto (Baliyan and Kumar 2016a), a few objective parameters measurable from the input ontology determine the complexity.

Unlike in OntoQA (Tartir and Arpinar 2007; Tartir et al. 2005), in ComplexOnto, the metrics are defined, regardless of it being populated with instances. Though there has been some research in design complexity of ontology, the area of structural complexity of ontology remains nascent and this chapter is aimed to quantify the difficulty level of given ontology.

In contrast to Swoogle's OntoRank (Sicilia et al. 2012), ComplexOnto has the advantage of removing duplicates and unreadable ontologies. The ontologies are ranked according to their goodness of use, which in turn is inversely related to complexity.

ComplexOnto's utility rests in it being easily computable and practical to apply. The weights assigned to ComplexOnto's components may be altered as per the relative significance of different facets of the ontology, rendering it a flexible measure. Additionally, the ComplexOnto score is not based on the Unified Model ing Language (UML) diagram, so it is not static. ComplexOnto score is based on the Web Ontology Language (OWL); it is continually updated on the Web.

Table 2.3 Comparative evaluation of ontology complexity metrics

Feature	Works that discuss complexity metrics					
	Kang et al. (2004)	Tartir et al. (2005), Tartir and Arpinar (2007)	Alani et al. (2006)	Yang et al. (2006)	Zhang (2010)	ComplexOnto
Is the metrics assessment objective?	Yes	Yes	Yes	Yes	Yes	Yes
Is there proper validation of proposed metrics?		Yes			Yes	Yes
Whether ontologies are ranked?		Yes				Yes
Whether the metrics flexible?	Yes					Yes
Whether the proposed metrics handle duplicates?				Yes	Yes	Yes

Zhang et al. (2010) measure design complexity of ontologies by extending the concept of software metrics. Their work could possibly be applied in ontology quality control and for managing ontology development projects, some of which lack validation.

Yang et al. (2006) demonstrate their metrics for ontology complexity on a domain ontology, namely Gene ontology; however, analytical validation is lacking for the same.

Table 2.3 presents a comparative analysis of OntoMod approach with aforesaid works (Baliyan and Kumar 2016a).

The impartiality of a complexity metric is achieved by being based on standard ontology artifacts. Flexibility points to user-assigned priorities for component metrics. Apart from the features seen in Table 2.3, ComplexOnto metrics may be applied to an unpopulated ontology, while other metrics such as Tartir and Arpinar (2007) need schema as well as instances.

2.5   Implementation

The cohesion and coupling values of a sample set of ontologies were computed using OntoMod and were contrasted with those computed using the models presented in Table 2.4. This shows the efficacy and correctness of OntoMod, especially in the cases where other models do not fare well or are simply inapplicable. Further, the

Table 2.4 Cohesion and coupling values for OntoMod and others

S. No.	Ontology		Metrics	
	Description	Visualization	OntoMod	(Ensan and Du 2013)
1	$S \sqsubseteq R \cup T$ $\exists L.T \sqsubseteq R$ $R \sqsubseteq P$ $Q \cap R \sqsubseteq P$		Cohesion = 0.37	Cohesion = 0.20
2.	$\exists L.Q \sqsubseteq P$ $R \sqsubseteq Q$ $S \sqsubseteq R$ $T \sqsubseteq S$		Cohesion = 0.53	Cohesion = 0.23
3.	Disconnected links $\exists L.Q \sqsubseteq P$ $S \sqsubseteq R$		Coupling = 1.33k	Coupling = k
4.	$P \sqsubseteq Q_1 \cap Q_2 \cap Q_3 \cap Q_4 \cap Q_5$ $R_1 \cup R_2 \cup R_3 \sqsubseteq P$		Cohesion = 0.43	Cohesion = 0.15
5.	$P \sqsubseteq Q_1 \cup Q_2 \cup Q_3 \cup Q_4 \cup Q_5$ $R_1 \cap R_2 \cap R_3 \sqsubseteq P$		Cohesion = 0.12	Cannot handle these cases

extensiveness of the model is confirmed through its ability to handle a variety of ontology structures.

The five ontologies on which OntoMod is implemented in Table 2.4 are partial real-world ontologies, visualized through dependence graphs. They are comprehensive in the sense that they exhibit every potential relationship type, i.e., union, and intersection, with universal, and existential quantifiers (Kumar et al. 2017).

Table 2.5 'Paper' ontologies and ComplexOnto's metrics

Ontology	ComplexOnto
Ont_1	10.132
Ont_2	7.063
Ont_3	129.896
Ont_4	58.766
Ont_5	10.619

Coupling implies inter-modular dependencies, thereby decreasing the self-sufficiency of a module; thus, a low value of coupling is desirable. In addition, the links with high sf indicate a high degree of dependency and hence high coupling. Ontology 3 has a weak and a strong inter-modular link, each. Ensan and Du's (2013) model categorizes links as: strong and moderate, so the weights used by them for normalization are different. Consequently, their values for coupling are distinct from OntoMod's. Even though the visualizations of ontology 4 and 5 are similar, yet the strengths of their dependencies and hence their sf s vary. Every link in ontology 4 represents total subsumption, so the corresponding direct links have strong dependency. On the contrary, ontology 5 deals with the various special cases mentioned in Sect. 2.3.1, so its dependencies fall in moderate and weak zones. Since the value of sf is directly proportional to cohesion, ontology 4 should have higher cohesion than the ontology 5. The model of Ensan and Du (2013) is capable of measuring the cohesion value for ontology 4, as it involves strong subsumption links, but the cohesion value is lesser than expected because their model does not handle transitive dependencies. Here, the ontology 4 has 15 transitive dependencies which are ignored by (Ensan and Du 2013). Moreover, ontology 5 includes multiple concepts in union or intersection. Such a case cannot be handled by the work of (Ensan and Du 2013). On the contrary, OntoMod handles strong dependencies of ontology 4 and multiple concepts' dependencies of ontology 5. Hence, the cohesion value of ontology 4 is higher than that of ontology 5.

In order to demonstrate the implementation of OntoMod's complexity metrics, i.e., ComplexOnto, we retrieve ontologies (.owl or .rdf) from keyword search on 'paper' on Swoogle (Finin et al. 2004). Table 2.5 gives values for ComplexOnto and its constituent metrics as defined in Sect. 2.3.2, for top 5 ontologies (Ont_1 to Ont_5) from Baliyan and Kumar (2016a).

The ranking of ontologies O_1 to O_5 by expert users and OntoQA have been taken from (Tartir and Arpinar 2007) and compared with Swoogle rankings in Table 2.6.

Then, we compute Spearman's rank-order correlation coefficient (ρ) for the rankings of Table 2.6. Results reveal a moderate positive correlation ($\rho = 0.5$) between the popularity of ontology (shown by Swoogle) and ComplexOnto metrics. Ontologies having less complexity are more popular than those with more complexity. Moreover, ComplexOnto overcomes the limitation of Swoogle to assign ranks to duplicates of ontology located at different Web addresses, by allocating same complexity scores and hence same ranks to duplicate ontologies.

Table 2.6 Ontology rankings by different methods

Ontology	Swoogle	ComplexOnto
Ont_1	1	2
Ont_2	2	1
Ont_3	3	5
Ont_4	4	4
Ont_5	5	3

Table 2.7 Calculation of ρ

Ontology	Swoogle rank	ComplexOnto rank	Difference of ranks (d)	Absolute difference ($|d|$)
Po_1	1	3	−2	2
Po_2	2	1	1	1
Po_3	3	10	−7	7
Po_4	4	7	−3	3
Po_5	5	15	−10	10
Po_6	6	9	−3	3
Po_7	7	2	5	5
Po_8	8	4	4	4
Po_9	9	8	1	1
Po_{10}	10	11	−1	1
Po_{11}	11	6	5	5
Po_{12}	12	12	0	0
Po_{13}	13	13	0	0
Po_{14}	14	5	9	9
Po_{15}	15	14	1	1

$\sum d^2 = 322, \quad 6 \times \sum d^2 = 1932, \quad n^3 - n = 3360, \quad \rho = 0.425$

Further, we retrieve ontologies (.owl or .rdf) from keyword search on 'phd' in Swoogle (Finin et al. 2004). Top 15 ontologies Po_1 to Po_{15}, as shown in Baliyan and Kumar (2016a), have been included. Table 2.6 shows the ranking of ontologies by Swoogle and ComplexOnto. The coefficient ρ is attained for the rankings, and its critical value is referred to. The value 0.425 in Table 2.7 specifies that there is a probability of 0.05 that the result is a matter of chance (Myers and Sirois 2004).

It can be seen from Fig. 2.8 that the absolute difference between the ranks generated by Swoogle and ComplexOnto for the 15 ontologies is small in most of the cases and a positive correlation is revealed between both from Table 2.7. This observation agrees with the instinct that the ontologies with lower complexity are more popular than those with higher complexity.

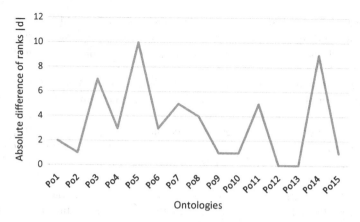

Fig. 2.8 Difference of ranks for ontologies

2.6 Conclusion and Summary

This chapter discusses two classes of ontology modularity metrics, structural and behavioral. While the former category includes complexity, cohesion, and coupling of a modular structure, providing an understanding of the efficiency of the modularization method, the latter category includes knowledge encapsulation, coverage of concepts and relationships, and depth of subsumption hierarchy, providing an understanding of the knowledge embedded in ontology as a whole. Here, we present a comprehensive definition of cohesion and coupling of modularized ontology. Further, the literature has been analyzed for relevant metrics in a modular ontology that characterize its behavior, determined through its embedded knowledge. Knowledge encapsulation, relationship and concept coverage, and depth of subsumption hierarchy have been included as important criteria for assessing the modular ontology's behavior that determines its parent SWA. This overall metrics suite for modular ontology quality is called OntoMod.

The specific research contributions of OntoMod are:

- It is an enhancement of the older works as it employs a continuous scale to handle the subtle variation in the strength of relationships.
- It infers indirect links that may not be apparent in the ontology structure. Additionally, OntoMod clearly defines rules to identify the strength of various dependency types.
- Standard validation frameworks have been applied to OntoMod to establish its correctness. Additionally, the metric values for sample ontologies have been confirmed to be more accurate than those of existing similar works.
- OntoMod facilitates the selection among alternative design principles in order to reduce coupling between partial ontologies (modules) and increase cohesion within the partial ontology (modules). This provides benefits of lower maintenance time and cost.

- OntoMod cohesion and coupling metrics handle the intensity (degree of dependence) as well as the type of the link between concepts. Experimental results confirm that they are more complete in terms of their capability to handle more features of ontology links.
- The framework uses a continuous and normalized ratio scale to quantify the quality of modular ontology, which enables the measurement of subtle differences in type of links.
- ComplexOnto does not skew results based on user weights and rather quantifies the structural quality of ontology. Moreover, the constituent ComplexOnto metrics exploit the information given by ontology editors which may be of some help to the ontology designer.
- Comparative empirical analysis on public domain ontologies has also been performed, and the rankings are found to be in line with those obtained from Swoogle.
- Our measures are unambiguous and may be applied to any type of ontology, such as cross-domain, domain, application, or task ontology in order to facilitate the assessment of quality of ontology or a partition thereof. The OntoMod suite calculates the overall quality of ontology after performing a weighted sum of the components, i.e., structural (cohesion, coupling, and complexity) and behavioral metrics.

Building on the quality evaluation of ontologies which form an integral part of SWAs, next chapter (Chap. 3) is dedicated toward the overall quality evaluation of SWAs. Such evaluation gives an abstract view of the SWA's quality to the user as opposed to ontology quality as desired by the ontology designer.

References

Abbès, S.B., Scheuermann, A., Meilender, T., d'Aquin, M.: Characterizing modular ontologies. In: Proceedings of the 7th International Conference on Formal Ontologies in Information Systems, pp. 13–25 (2012)

Alani, H., Christopher, B., Nigel, S.: Ranking ontologies with AKTiveRank. In: Proceedings of the 5th International Semantic Web Conference. Springer, Berlin, pp. 1–15 (2006)

Baliyan, N., Kumar, S.: Software process and quality evaluation for semantic web applications. IETE Tech. Rev. **31**(6), 452–462 (2014)

Baliyan, N., Kumar, S.: Towards measurement of structural complexity for ontologies. Int. J. Web Eng. Technol. **11**(2), 153–173 (2016)

Baliyan, N., Kumar, S.: A behavioral metrics suite for modular ontologies. In: Proceedings of the Second International Conference on Information and Communication Technology for Competitive Strategies, p. 133. ACM (2016b)

Barksdale Jr., J.B.: Sets and Randolph Diagrams. Available online at https://files.eric.ed.gov/fullte xt/ED045458.pdf. Last accessed Jan 2018 (October 1970)

Bateman, J., Borgo, S., Lüttich, K., Masolo, C., Mossakowski, T.: Ontological modularity and spatial diversity. Spat. Cogn. Comput. **7**(1), 97–128 (2007)

Breitman, K., Casanova, M.A., Truszkowski, W.: Semantic Web: Concepts, Technologies and Applications. Springer Science & Business Media, Berlin (2007)

Briand, L.C., Morasca, S., Basili, V.R.: Property-based software engineering measurement. IEEE Trans. Software Eng. **22**(1), 68–86 (1996)

Duque-Ramos, A., Fernández-Breis, J.T., Iniesta, M., Dumontier, M., Egaña, Aranguren M., Schulz, S., Stevens, R.: Evaluation of the OQuaRE framework for ontology quality. Expert Syst. Appl. **40**(7), 2696–2703 (2013)

Ensan, F., Du, W.: A modular approach to scalable ontology development. In: Canadian Semantic Web: Technologies and Applications, pp. 79–103 (2010)

Ensan, F., Du, W.: A semantic metrics suite for evaluating modular ontologies. Inf. Syst. **38**(5), 745–770 (2013)

Evermann, J., Fang, J.: Evaluating ontologies: towards a cognitive measure of quality. Inf. Syst. **35**(4), 391–403 (2010)

Finin, T., Reddivari, P., Cost, R.S., Sachs, J.: Swoogle: a search and metadata engine for the semantic web. In: Proceedings of the ACM Conference on Information and Knowledge Management, pp. 652–659 (2004)

García, J., García, F., Therón, R.: Defining coupling metrics among classes in an OWL ontology. In: Lecture Notes in Computer Science, vol. 6097, pp. 12–17. Springer, Berlin (2010a)

García, J., García, F., Therón, R.: Visualising semantic coupling among entities in an owl ontology. In: Lecture notes in business information processing. Springer, Berlin, vol. 62, pp. 90–106 (2010b)

Hlomani, H., Stacey, D.: Approaches, methods, metrics, measures, and subjectivity in ontology evaluation: a survey. Semant. Web J. 1–5 (2014)

IEEE, IEEE STD 1061-1998: IEEE Standard for a Software Quality Metrics Methodology. http://ieeexplore.ieee.org/xpl/articleDetails.jsp?arnumber=749159 (1998)

Kang, D., Xu, B., Lu, J., Chu, W.C.: A complexity measure for ontology based on UML. In: Proceedings of the IEEE 10th International Workshop on Future Trends of Distributed Computing Systems, pp. 222–228 (2004)

Khan, Z. C.: Evaluation metrics in ontology modules. In: 29th International Workshop on Description Logics (DL 2016), CEUR Workshop Proceedings, vol. 1577, Cape Town, South Africa. CEUR-WS.org, 22–25 April 2016

Kumar, S., Baliyan, N., Sukalikar, S.: Ontology cohesion and coupling metrics. Int. J. Semant. Web Inf. Syst. (IJSWIS) **13**(4), 1–26 (2017)

Ma, Y., Jin, B., Feng, Y.: Semantic oriented ontology cohesion metrics for ontology-based systems. J. Syst. Softw. **83**(1), 143–152 (2010)

McCabe, T.J.: A complexity measure. IEEE Trans. Softw. Eng. **2**(4), 308–320 (1976)

Myers, L., Sirois, M. J.: Spearman correlation coefficients, differences between. In: Kotz, S., Read, C.B., Balakrishnan, N., Vidakovic, B., Johnson, N.L. (eds.), Encyclopedia of Statistical Sciences, vol. 12. Wiley, Hoboken (2004)

Narasimhan, V.L., Hendradjaya, B.: Some theoretical considerations for a suite of metrics for the integration of software components. Inf. Sci. J. **177**(3), 844–864 (2007)

Oh, S., Yeom, H.Y., Ahn, J.: Cohesion and coupling metrics for ontology modules. Inf. Technol. Manag. J. **12**(2), 81–96 (2011)

Orme, A.M., Tao, H., Etzkorn, L.H.: Coupling metrics for ontology-based system. IEEE Softw. **23**(2), 102–108 (2006)

Ouyang, L., Zou, B., Qu, M., Zhang, C.: A method of ontology evaluation based on coverage, cohesion and coupling. In: Proceedings of the 8th International Conference on Fuzzy Systems Knowledge Discovery, pp. 2451–2455 (2011)

Pressman, R. S.: Software Engineering: A Practitioner's Approach, 6th International ed., p. 388. McGraw-Hill (2005)

Sicilia, M.A., Rodríguez, D., Barriocanal, E.G., Alonso, S.S.: Empirical findings on ontology metrics. Expert Syst. Appl. **39**(8) (2012)

Stvilia, B.: A model for ontology quality evaluation. First Monday, **12**(12) (2007)

Sukalikar, S., Kumar, S., Baliyan, N.: Analysing cohesion and coupling for modular ontologies. In: 2014 International Conference on Advances in Computing, Communications and Informatics (ICACCI), pp. 2063–2066. IEEE (2014)

Tartir, S., Arpinar, I.B.: Ontology evaluation and ranking using OntoQA. In: Proceedings of the IEEE International Conference on Semantic Computing, pp. 185–192 (2007)

Tartir, S., Arpinar, I.B., Moore, M., Sheth, A.P., Meza, B.A.: OntoQA: metric-based ontology quality analysis. In: Proceedings of the IEEE Workshop on Knowledge Acquisition from Distributed, Autonomous, Semantically Heterogeneous Data and Knowledge Sources (2005)

Verma, A.: An abstract framework for ontology evaluation. In: 2016 International Conference on Data Science and Engineering (ICDSE), Cochin, pp. 1–6 (2016)

Vrandečić, D., Sure, Y.: How to design better ontology metrics. Semant. Web Res. Appl. **4519**, 311–325 (2007)

Yang, Z., Zhang, D., Ye, C.: Evaluation metrics for ontology complexity and evolution analysis. In: Proceedings of the IEEE International Conference on E-Business Engineering, pp. 162–170 (2006)

Yao, H., Orme, A.M., Etzkorn, L.: Cohesion metrics for ontology design and application. J. Comput. Sci. **1**(1), 107–113 (2005)

Zhang, H., Li, Y.F., Tan, H.B.K.: Measuring design complexity of semantic web ontologies. J. Syst. Softw. **83**(5), 803–814 (2010)

Zhu, H., Liu, D., Bayley, I., Aldea, A., Yang, Y., Chen, Y.: Quality model and metrics of ontology for semantic descriptions of web services. Tsinghua Sci. Technol. **22**(3), 254–272 (2017)

Chapter 3
Quality Evaluation of Semantic Web Applications

Abstract As discussed in Chap. 1, Semantic Web applications are radically changing the software industry through their ability to share and use data from heterogeneous sources. This in turn enables the discovery of meaningful relationships among chunks of data. Having understood the significance of such applications in giving insights into knowledge toward solving real-world problems, one must measure and improve their quality. This chapter carries forward the idea of assessing ontologies from Chap. 2 and underlines the need for assessing in totality, a Semantic Web application supported by ontology. This may benefit customer by providing his/her the quality ranking of different Semantic Web applications which provide similar functionality. Moreover, the developer may use the qualitative assessment result toward monitoring and improvising his Semantic Web application. As per our knowledge, there exists no framework which allows customers to rank Semantic Web applications based on their quality. It is expected of such framework to preserve the quality attributes of Semantic Web-based applications, which overlap with conventional software or Web applications and in addition incorporate specific quality attributes of Semantic Web-based applications. This chapter presents in detail a Semantic Web application quality evaluation framework (referred to as SWAQ) which employs Analytic Hierarchy Process for Multiple Criteria Decision-Making and Fuzzy Inference System for finding the quality. The implementation of SWAQ has been described using a case study, and comparative study of results has been done. Moreover, SWAQ's foundations have been validated with the help of standard benchmarks of IEEE 1061 and Kitchenham.

Keywords Semantic Web application · Analytic Hierarchy Process
Fuzzy Inference System · Quality

Section 3.1 discusses the challenges faced while attempting the qualitative assessment of Semantic Web applications (SWAs) and explains the motivation behind SWAQ. Section 3.2 outlines existing work in this field and summarizes some notable quality models for software and Web applications. It then enlists the adapted and new quality attributes. Next, Sect. 3.3 presents SWAQ metrics suite in detail, where Sect. 3.3.1 explains Analytic Hierarchy Process (AHP) for ranking SWAs, while

© The Author(s) 2018
S. Kumar and N. Baliyan, *Semantic Web-Based Systems*, SpringerBriefs in Computer
Science, https://doi.org/10.1007/978-981-10-7700-5_3

Sect. 3.3.2 describes Fuzzy Inference System (FIS) for the same purpose. Section 3.4 presents the conceptual validation of SWAQ through IEEE 1061 criteria and Kitchenham's framework. Section 3.5 asserts that the implementation of SWAQ is relatively superior and encompasses more dimensions than existing works in this field. Section 3.6 concludes the chapter.

3.1 Semantic Web Application Quality

The innovation called Semantic Web hopes for the refinement of present form of the World Wide Web, through machine-comprehendible data. This data may be understood, found, and combined without manual intervention. Furthermore, machine readability of data empowers programmed annotation of metadata to current Web documents. However, SWAs contrast with Web applications from various aspects—openness, computational difficulty, Web semantics' ambiguity, and manageability, to name a few. Overall, SWAs are advantageous in the sense that they permit interoperability and reuse among Web applications, which leads to better efficiency and condensed development life cycle and cost (W3C 2014).

> ISO defines software quality as the "degree to which the software product satisfies stated and implied needs, when used under specified conditions" (Azuma 2001).

Traditional quality evaluation approaches for software, and Web applications discard certain attributes pertinent to SWAs' quality. Additionally, these approaches consider certain attributes, which are either superfluous for SWAs or whose metrics need adaptation to suit SWAs' measurement (Bernstein 2011).

While developing a ranking framework for SWAs' quality, multiple issues arise. Firstly, it may be infeasible to measure some SWA quality attributes even through indirect measures (Baliyan and Kumar 2013a, 2014). SWAQ consists of SWA quality attributes and sub-attributes, wherever applicable. These quality attributes are obtained after adaptation of available software and Web application quality attributes available in the literature. In addition, unique attributes of SWAs have been recognized. Further, SWAQ formulates direct or indirect measures for the listed quality attributes, with the help of the Goal Question Metric (GQM) methodology (Solingen and Berghout 1999).

The second issue is to define SWA quality in an unbiased way. Although the quality attributes may have been quantified, their exact association with SWA quality is difficult to estimate. Hence, SWAQ employs a FIS, which integrates a rule set and tackles the fuzziness in SWA attributes' measurement in order to decide SWA quality (Jang and Gulley 1995). The developers may utilize SWAQ for observing and improving their SWA's quality. At the same time, SWA consumers may match SWAQ value with the value specified in Quality of Service (QoS) file of a SWA.

Another issue faced in assessment of SWAs is ranking of SWA alternatives, as per user-assigned priorities for quality attributes. With the availability of multiple SWA options that achieve the same goal, a user frequently finds it difficult to make a choice; for instance, the choice among semantic search facility providers, namely, DuckDuckGo, sindice, sensebot etc. (HLWIKI 2015). SWAQ resolves this through AHP, a Multiple Criteria Decision-Making (MCDM) method (Saaty 2000).

3.2 Overview of Some Works on Quality Evaluation of Semantic Web Applications

Table 3.1 summarizes standard software quality models (Pressman 2001).

SWAQ discusses quality attributes by adapting some standard quality attributes of software as well as Web applications, which the SWAs retain. Additionally, some unique characteristics of SWAs that determine their quality have been included. We found an overlap of some quality attributes across different quality models. Furthermore, some quality attributes feature as sub-attributes in another quality model. These overlapping and subsumed attributes are accounted for, only once for consistency's sake during the adaptation of quality models for SWAs.

In Table 3.1, functional suitability is common to ISO/IEC 25010 and ISO/IEC 9126 as functionality (Pressman 2001). ISO/IEC 9126's functionality subsumes ISO/IEC 25010's security. ISO/IEC 25010's maintainability subsumes McCall's reusability. Similarly, Boehm's testability, modifiability, and understandability are contained in the maintainability attribute. In Table 3.1 the quality attributes of the most recent ISO/IEC 25010 model (i.e., functionality) alongside the quality attributes defined in almost all of the above-mentioned models (i.e., efficiency, maintainability, portability, reliability, and reusability) are chosen to become a part of the SWAQ framework.

Table 3.1 Software quality models and their attributes

Quality models (Pressman 2001)	Attributes handled by the model
Boehm	Efficiency, human engineering, testability, modifiability, understandability, portability, reliability, testability
McCall	Correctness, efficiency, flexibility, integrity, interoperability, reusability, portability, reliability, testability, usability
ISO/IEC 9126	Efficiency, functionality, maintainability, portability, reliability, usability
ISO/IEC 25010	Compatibility, performance efficiency, functional suitability, security, maintainability, operability, portability, reliability, transferability, usability

Moreover, precision and recall form the measures of efficiency of a SWA, as discussed later in this section. Since maintenance accounts for majority of the effort in software development life cycle, therefore, maintainability significantly determines quality (Koch 2004). Portability or compatibility with all operating systems assumed an intrinsic attribute for SWAs, given their compatibility with browsers. Further, SWA's reliability is different from software's reliability and is defined through provenance later in this section. Usability is shared among all quality models and is pertinent to the SWAs having a query/response interface for users. To sum up, the quality attributes retained from software quality models are *functionality, maintainability, and usability.*

Traditional software usually has a restricted number of users at any point in time, whereas a Web application should accommodate increasing number of users for consideration as a high-quality application (Mich et al. 2003). SWAs are in essence Web applications whose use is expected to grow with time; hence, scalability is included as a quality attribute in SWAQ. A majority of Web application quality attributes have already been included as software attributes in SWAQ, so the sole quality attribute taken from Web applications' quality is *scalability.*

Table 3.2 summarizes quality models and attributes available for Web applications.

Table 3.3 summarizes earlier attempts at assessing SWA quality, most of which offer a theoretical model, while a few formulate quality metrics for SWAs.

A crucial facet during assimilation of data from multiple dissimilar sources is its provenance, which indicates the roots of data and sometimes the processing or reasoning operations permissible on that data. Provenance is essential to SWA quality because it affects the SWA's reliability. Precision and recall affect the reliability of SWAs, which provide search facility. Additionally, availability finds a place in SWAQ as it widely encompasses accessibility and query response time (as shown in Table 3.3). Hence, the quality attributes adapted from SWA quality are *provenance, precision, recall,* and *availability.*

3.3 A Quality Evaluation Model for Semantic Web Applications

The Semantic Web application quality (SWAQ) framework discussed by Baliyan and Kumar (2018) is multifaceted as it includes GQM, AHP, and FIS elements. Users may choose among SWA options based on their quality ranking, whereas the developers may monitor the quality value for a given SWA in order to better it. Figure 3.1 shows the outline of SWAQ framework.

Table 3.2 Quality models for Web applications and their attributes

Reference	Model	Attribute	Description
Mich et al. (2003)	Right weight	Scalability Flexibility	– The capability to allow a growing number of users – Changeability; sub-attribute of maintainability
Marsico and Levialdi (2004)	COFUE	Social quality Information on site Communication style	– No metrics defined – Quality data is questionnaire-based; not objective – User point of view considered – Sub-attribute of aesthetics and affects usability
Calero et al. (2005)	WQM	Usability Operation Presentation Maintenance	– Ease of learning and use – Sub-attribute of functionality – Sub-attribute of usability – Sub-attribute of maintainability
Signore (2005)	Signore model	Correctness Content Presentation Navigation Interaction	– Consistency of execution with documentation – Same as rich content; sub-attribute of usability – Same as aesthetics; sub-attribute of usability – Same as aesthetics; sub-attribute of usability – Same as aesthetics; sub-attribute of usability
Zhou (2009)	WEF	Ease of use Aesthetics Multimedia Rich content Reputation	– Same as usability – Look and feel; sub-attribute of usability – Video/audio content; sub-attribute of usability – Bulletin, search, etc.; sub-attribute of usability – Trust, publicity, etc.; sub-attribute of usability

As seen in Fig. 3.1, SWAQ metrics are formularized from corresponding attributes, to begin with. The method followed for this purpose is GQM. Further, the SWAQ attributes may be customized to suit user's requirements for a particular SWA. Secondly, the AHP and FIS component take these metric values as input. AHP outputs the relative ordering of SWAs on quality basis, while FIS outputs overall quality value and the ranking among alternative SWAs is obtained. Subsequently, the SWA with the maximum value of quality is selected for use.

SWAQ exhibits a twofold setting, first, AHP-based SWA rankings and second FIS-based SWAQ values followed by rankings. The fuzzy system method is apt for SWA selection since the ambiguity in values of SWAs' quality attributes is tackled

Table 3.3 Existing quality models for Semantic Web application quality models and their attributes

Reference	Attribute	Sub-attribute	Description of attribute	Whether the measure is direct?
Pusnik et al. (2013)	Usability	Ease of use	Ease of querying and updating	Yes
Zaveri et al. (2013)		Accessibility	Is there a need for user registration?	Yes
Zaveri et al. (2013)	Performance	Data structure	Transforming unstructured data to structured data (same as extensibility)	No
		Extensibility	Liberty to annotate semantic links with ease; same as maintainability	No
		Query response	Delay between time of firing query and time of receiving first response	Yes
Mendes et al. (2012)	Representational quality	Completeness	Is all relevant data included? (same as recall)	Yes
		Recall	Part of data, which is relevant and is retrieved	Yes
Mendes et al. (2012)	Contextual quality	Conciseness	Is there no redundant data? (same as precision)	Yes
		Precision	Part of retrieved data, which is relevant	Yes
Mendes et al. (2012)	Provenance	Consistency	The absence of contradictory values	Yes
Pusnik et al. (2013)		Expert's role	Domain experts' role in marking semantics	No

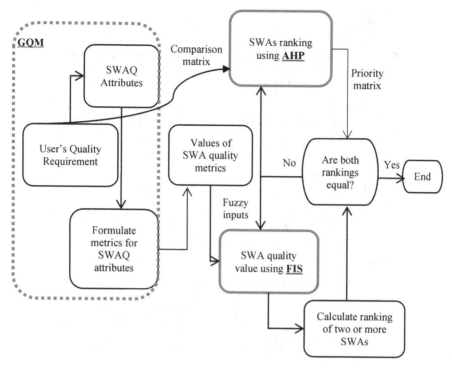

Fig. 3.1 SWAQ framework

through rules in the fuzzy inference system, whereas AHP achieves SWA ranking through comparison of quality attributes' values for SWAs. One should receive feedback from domain expert while creating a rule-base in FIS. The AHP component is apt when there are several SWA alternatives available, since AHP employs pairwise comparison approach for tackling subjectivity and the absence of expertise. Either FIS or AHP may be implemented depending on the situation, i.e., use FIS when precise values of quality attributes are unknown; however, the inference rules are accessible. On the other hand, use AHP when comparative weights among quality attributes are accessible. In other words, FIS is suitable when an expert user is available, while AHP is suitable even for naïve users. We now summarize the components devised for and steps followed in use of the SWAQ framework. In particular, GQM for quality attribute selection and attribute to metric mapping, AHP for ranking SWAs, and FIS to attain a discrete SWAQ value for SWAs is defined.

SWAQ

A: set of SWA alternatives, $A = \{a_1, ..., a_n\}$
G :{measurement sub goals revised from current quality models, or recognized as characteristics of SWAs}
1.   for each sub goal s, s.t. s ε G
               obtain 's to metric' mapping
2.   for each a, s.t. a ε A
               using s values, do pairwise comparisons, i.e., $a_1 || a_2, a_1 || a_3$ etc.
3.   AHP output:
               Quality based SWAs' ranking
4.   FIS inputs:
               s values
5.   FIS output:
               SWA quality
6.   for each a, s.t. a ε A
               find SWA quality
               find SWA ranking ($\propto \frac{1}{SWA\ quality}$)

GQM

1.   Consider sub-attributes in set G, only once.
2.   for each s ε G
         characterize the measurement entity through contextual queries.
         using the queries, formulate a direct or indirect measure of s
                     if s is immeasurable
                               obtain user or expert's feedback
                     else
                               define metric for s ranging between 0 and 1
         if s is not applicable to a SWA
                     assign it a 0 value

AHP

1.   Pick the top level goal, i.e., SWA quality
2.   Find SWA alternatives in a domain
3.   Using formulations of GQM,
               do pairwise comparisons of s
4.   for each populated comparison matrix
               normalize the matrix and obtain ranking vector
5.   Rank alternatives based on SWA quality

FIS

1.   Prepare rule base based on expert's inputs and/or logical inference
2.   Input:
               s values from GQM
3.   Choose defuzzification method
4.   Output:
               defuzzified output is SWA quality

SWAQ attributes are decided after modification of software's, Web application's, and SWA's quality attributes, as discussed earlier. Currently, there is no openly available metric or methodology to define exclusive SWA attributes. SWAQ is an innovative effort of Baliyan and Kumar (2018) in this field. SWAQ is easy to understand since all its metrics adhere to the ratio scale of measurement, without any units; moreover, the metrics fall in the range of 0–1. In the following paragraphs, we formularize SWAQ's metrics with the help of GQM method.

Maintainability

The IEEE standard definition of maintainability is, "the ease with which a software system or component can be modified to correct faults, improve performance or other attributes, or adapt to a changed environment (Coleman et al. 1998)."

Here, the measurement goal is easy and dynamic updation of SWA's versions, and the question asked is how easy is it to maintain a given SWA. The formulation of maintainability is consequential from a highly popular work of Coleman et al. (1998), in which a maintainability index (m) ranges from 0 to 100; hence, maintainability M in SWAQ model is normalized by (3.1). The measure is pertinent since maintainability of a SWA is essentially defined in the same way as that of software.

$$M = m/100 \qquad (3.1)$$

where

$$m = 171 - 3.42\ln(\text{aveE}) - 0.23\text{aveV}(g')$$
$$- 16.2\ln(\text{aveLOC}) + (50 \times (\sin(\text{sqrt}(2.46 \times \text{aveCM}))))$$

aveE	Average effort per module
aveV(g')	Average extended cyclomatic complexity per module
aveLOC	Average numbers of lines of code per module
aveCM	Average cyclomatic complexity

Functionality

The function point metric may be successfully employed to gauge the functionality delivered by a system (Abrahao and Oscar 2003). A Web application and hence SWAs vary from software with respect to the elements of Unadjusted Function Point Count (UFC) (Abrahao and Oscar 2003). Here, the goal is to achieve a rich set of functional concepts of SWA, and the question asked is how much functionality is provided by the SWA to its user. As UFC and Value Adjustment Factor (VAF) εR^+, the normalized functionality, F, is defined by (3.2).

$$F = \begin{cases} \text{UFC} \times \text{VAF}, & \text{UFC} \leq 1 \text{ and VAF} \leq 1 \\ (\text{UFC} \times \text{VAF})/(\max(\text{UFC, VAF}))^2, & \text{otherwise} \end{cases} \qquad (3.2)$$

where

$$\text{UFC} = \sum_{i=1}^{5}\sum_{j=1}^{3} w_{ij}, C_{ij}$$

w_{ij} Weight of the ith functionality, at jth complexity
C_{ij} Complexity of the ith functionality, at jth complexity

$$\text{VAF} = 0.65 + 0.01 \sum_{i=1}^{14} F_i$$

F_i Degree of influence of ith functionality on a scale of 0–5

Scalability

Scalability can be categorized into horizontal (h_s) and vertical (v_s) scalability (Mich et al. 2003). H_s is the capability to grow in breadth, and the goal is to add maximum number of links in an ontology. The question asked is how rich can an ontology grow in links (Mich et al. 2003). H_s is computed as the number of potential links or Uniform Resource Indicators (URIs) divided by the number of existing links, as in (3.3).

$$h_s = \# \text{ added links or URIs}/\# \text{ links} \tag{3.3}$$

Moreover, v_s is the capability to grow in height, and the goal is to add maximum number of namespaces to an ontology (Mich et al. 2003). The question asked is how many ontologies can still be added. It is computed as the number of potential namespaces divided by the number of existing namespaces, as in (3.4).

$$v_s = \# \text{ added namespaces}/\# \text{ namespaces} \tag{3.4}$$

Since h_s and $v_s \varepsilon R^+$, the normalized scalability, S, is defined by (3.5). In cases where one of the 'additional links' and 'additional namespaces' is more significant than the other, the weights may be inclined away from 0.5, accordingly.

$$S = \begin{cases} 0.5h_s + 0.5v_s, & h_s \leq 1 \text{ and } v_s \leq 1 \\ 0.5 \times \{h_s/\max(h_s, v_s)\} + 0.5 \times \{v_s/\max(h_s, v_s)\}, & \text{otherwise} \end{cases} \tag{3.5}$$

Usability

Usability is an indirect quality measure; therefore, it is expressed in terms of a user's score of his/her *know-how* of the SWA. The goal is to achieve a gradual learning curve for the user. The question raised is how eye-catching the SWA is for use by an average user. The number of times a SWA has been used by a particular user should be noted while finding user's score for that SWA, because only someone who has used the SWA enough deserves to assess it. To this end, we categorize users as naïve, average, and expert, and their scores are allotted confidence levels of 1, 2, and 3, respectively. The formula for usability, U, is given by (3.6).

$$U = u/u_c \qquad (3.6)$$

where

$$u = \sum_{i=1}^{n} c_i r_i / n$$

n Number of users
r_i Rating by ith user, from 0 to r_{max}
c_i Confidence in ith user

We may expand (3.6) to accommodate up to c_{max} user classes, which is also the maximum confidence level. On similar lines, the upper threshold of user rating may be expanded up to r_{max}. We define the usability constant u_c as $c_{max} \times r_{max}$.

Availability

The notion of availability, denoted by A, incorporates accessibility and query response time (Zaveri et al. 2013). A highly available SWA is anticipated as it will easily be accessible to the user; moreover, its response to user queries will be prompt. Therefore, the metric A has two components, i.e., up ratio and response time lag. For up ratio, the goal is to be up and running whenever user tries to access it. Further, the question while determining up ratio is how many times while attempting access is SWA available (Zaveri et al. 2013). Up ratio is given in (3.7).

$$\text{up ratio} = \frac{\text{number of times SWA is available}}{\text{number of times SWA is accessed}} \qquad (3.7)$$

For response time, the goal is that the SWA responds promptly to user requests and the question is what is the amount of lag between assured response time and real response time. Response time lag is defined in (3.8).

$$\text{rtlag} = \begin{cases} 0, & \text{rt lag}_{av} \leq \text{rtlag}_{max} \\ (\text{rtlag}_{av} - \text{rtlag}_{max})/\text{rtlag}_{max}, & \text{rtlag}_{max} < \text{rtlag}_{av} < 2 \times \text{rtlag}_{max} \\ 1, & \text{otherwise} \end{cases}$$

$$(3.8)$$

where

rtlag_{max} Maximum lag allowed in response time
rtlag_{av} Average response time

The times in (3.8) may be computed on system clock in uniform units. Also, if the values computed from (3.7) and (3.8) fall within [0, 1], A is defined by (3.9).

$$A = \begin{cases} 0, & \text{upratio} = 0 \text{ or rtlag} = 0 \\ \text{upratio} \times \text{rtlag}, & \text{otherwise} \end{cases} \tag{3.9}$$

Up ratio specifies the possibility of accessibility and ranges from 0 to 1, whereas response time lag is multiplied to quantify delayed responses if any.

Provenance

Prior to defining provenance, we must define F-measure, f_m, which consists of precision and recall (Mendes et al. 2012). Precision is the portion of recovered documents, which are relevant in the domain. The goal of precision is to achieve a 100% value; i.e., all recovered documents should be relevant (Mendes et al. 2012). Here, the question asked is: Are there too many recovered irrelevant results. Precision is measured as in (3.10).

$$P_r = \frac{(\text{number of relevant results} \cap \text{number of retrieved results})}{\text{number of retrieved results}} \tag{3.10}$$

where number of relevant results $\cap$ number of retrieved results $= \sum_{i=1}^{n} r_i c_i$

n Number of retrieved results
r_i Expert's degree of relevance for ith retrieved result
c_i Number of results with degree of relevance r_i

Recall is the portion of documents relevant to the query, which are successfully recovered. The goal of precision is to attain a 100% value, i.e., all relevant results should be recovered (Mendes et al. 2012). Here, the question asked is: Are there too many relevant results that are not recovered. Recall is measured as in (3.11).

$$R_e = \frac{(\text{number of relevant results} \cap \text{number of retrieved results})}{\text{number of relevant results}} \tag{3.11}$$

where the number of relevant results is the number of results anticipated with a standard or best known SWA of a similar domain as adjudged by domain experts. The F-measure is given by (3.12).

$$f_m = 2 \times (P_r \times R_e / P_r + R_e) \tag{3.12}$$

With pervasive and massive Semantic Web data, provenance or information regarding the roots of data assumes a significant role during the development of novel SWAs (W3C 2014). The goal is to gauge the integrity of data source, and the question asked is can the data dissemination source be trusted? If the SWA does not support search facility, F-measure is not applicable, and provenance is used instead

(Pusnik et al. 2013). Provenance is an indirect measure obtained as a user-assigned score. The normalized provenance, P, is given in (3.13).

$$P = p/p_{\max} \qquad\qquad (3.13)$$

where p is the rating given by users between 0 and $p_{\max}$.

3.3.1   Quality-Based Ranking Using Analytic Hierarchy Process

Various levels of SWAs' attribute nesting complicate the ranking procedure. This problem is known as MCDM, in which decision makers rank choices based on multiple criteria (Zeleny 1982). The common weighted sum approach is not applicable to a hierarchy of attributes, as in SWA's case. Additionally, some attributes may be quantified only indirectly and some not at all. The issue here is to compare each SWA based on each attribute, i.e., how to quantify and combine the attribute hierarchy into a meaningful metric.

AHP is a popular method for solving MCDM problems since it is flexible to allow any number of attributes and sub-attributes (Saaty 2008). AHP is based on pairwise comparisons of decision criteria instead of utility and weighing functions, which facilitates the decision maker to find trade-offs among criteria. Furthermore, AHP enables consistency check for assessment criteria and alternatives (Saaty 2008). AHP accommodates both subjective and objective evaluation measures, therefore decreasing prejudice at decision making.

One of the main offerings of the SWAQ framework is the SWA ranking, tailored to user's requirements. Basically, AHP component of SWAQ lets the user allocate weights to SWAs' quality attributes. Next, according to the weights and quality attribute values, SWAs are ranked in decreasing order of quality. Thus, for ranking SWAs based on multiple quality attributes, the steps are:

- Define a hierarchy of SWAs based on SWAQ attributes.
- Formulate comparison matrix for SWAQ attributes.
- Obtain comparison matrices of SWAs for each SWAQ attribute.
- Perform aggregation of comparisons in order to obtain SWA ranking.

These steps in AHP-based ranking of SWAQ are described in detail in the next sections using a case study.

Hierarchy of SWAs Based on SWAQ Attributes

Figure 3.2 shows the hierarchy of SWAQ attributes. The first layer is the goal of the analysis, i.e., to find the comparative SWAQ value for candidate SWAs that meet user's functional requirements. The subsequent layers up to the last comprise a hierarchy of functional and non-functional SWAQ attributes. The bottom layer

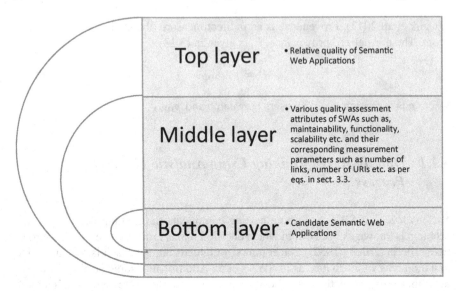

Fig. 3.2 AHP hierarchy

Table 3.4 Attribute
comparison matrix

	M	F	S	U	A	P
M	1	5	0.5	3	5	3
F	0.2	1	1	2	4	5
S	2	1	1	3	0.5	2
U	0.33	0.5	0.33	1	5	0.5
A	0.2	0.25	2	0.2	1	0.5
P	0.33	0.2	0.5	2	2	1

contains the SWAQ metrics' values obtained from intermediate layers, for each SWA
(Baliyan and Kumar 2018).

Comparison Matrix for SWAQ Attributes

For comparing different SWAs, one needs to allocate priorities to each attribute as per
their relative contribution in overall quality. The SWAQ attribute priorities could be
on a scale of 1–9 as suggested in the AHP method (Saaty 2008). The weights 1, 3, 5, 7,
and 9 represent equal, moderate, strong, very strong, and extreme degree of priority,
respectively, whereas the weights 2, 4, 6, and 8 on the preference scale represent
intermediate degree of priority, i.e., compensation between weights (Saaty 2008).
Moreover, in the matrix, for each a_{ij}, the entity a_{ji} indicates inverse comparison.
The attribute comparison matrix for our case study is in Table 3.4, where symbols
derive their meanings from Sect. 3.3.

Next, this matrix is squared, and the sum of each row is written as a column
vector. Each row of this column vector is divided by the sum of that column to

Table 3.5 Normalized priority matrix

	M	F	S	U	A	P	Row sum	Normalized priorities
M	6	13.85	18.5	24.5	51.25	36	150.1	0.3280
F	5.5333	6	13.2667	18.4	29.5	15.6	88.3	0.1929
S	5.9667	14.025	6	18.1	34	16.75	94.8417	0.2072
U	2.6	4.35	11.5833	6	14.8333	7.6667	47.0333	0.1028
A	4.6833	3.7	4.6667	8.5	6	6.95	34.5	0.0754
P	2.7733	4.0667	6.0333	7.3	16.7167	6	42.89	0.0937
						Total	457.665	1

Table 3.6 Input values for SWAQ attributes

SWAs	SWA_x	SWA_y	SWA_z
M	0.4211	0.5669	0.3294
F	0.7469	0.1986	0.9161
S	0.4515	0.2587	0.3164
U	0.8126	0.8216	0.9067
A	0.305	0.7238	0.6722
P	0.1696	0.7848	0.839

get the normalized value of the corresponding SWAQ attribute. Also, the sum of priorities assigned to SWAQ attributes must be 1 as shown in Table 3.5.

Therefore, based on the normalized priorities the relative ranking of SWAQ attributes is: $A < P < U < F < S < M$.

Comparison Matrices of SWAs for Each SWAQ Attribute

In this case study, random values for each SWAQ attribute of SWAs (SWA_x, SWA_y, and SWA_z) are shown in Table 3.6; they lie in (0, 1]. The comparison matrix for maintainability, M, is obtained as $c_{ij} = a_{1i}/a_{1j}$, where a_{ij} are the cells of the matrix in Table 3.6, e.g., $c_{12} = a_{11}/a_{12} = 0.4211/0.5669$. So, $c_{12} = 0.7428$.

We obtain comparison matrix for each SWAQ attribute in this fashion. Next, this matrix is squared, and the sum of each row is written as a column vector. Each row of this column vector is divided by the sum of that column to get the normalized value of M for each SWA. Also, the sum of priorities of M assigned to SWAQ attributes must be 1 as shown in Table 3.7.

Aggregation of Comparisons for SWA Ranking

With the application of above-mentioned approach, the normalized priorities of all SWAQ attributes for SWAs are obtained. These may be used to form an aggregate comparison matrix as in Table 3.8, which is subsequently multiplied by the normalized priority matrix of quality attribute to obtain SWAs' quality ranking.

The product of 3×6 and 6×1 matrices juxtaposed in Table 3.8 is a 3×1 matrix as shown in Table 3.9.

Table 3.7 Priority matrix for SWAs for M

Comparison matrix for SWAs			Squared matrix				
	SWA_x	SWA_y	SWA_z	SWA_x	SWA_y	SWA_z	Row sum	Normalized priority
SWA_x	1	0.7428	1.2786	3	2.2285	3.8359	9.0644	0.3197
SWA_y	1.3462	1	1.7213	4.0387	3	5.1640	12.2027	0.4303
SWA_z	0.7821	0.5809	1	2.3462	1.7428	3	7.0891	0.2500

Table 3.8 Aggregate comparison and criteria ranking

	M	F	S	U	A	P	Criteria ranking
SWA_x	0.3197	0.4012	0.4398	0.3198	0.1793	0.0946	0.3280
SWA_y	0.4303	0.1067	0.2520	0.3234	0.4255	0.4376	0.1929
SWA_z	0.2500	0.4921	0.3082	0.3568	0.3952	0.4678	0.2072
							0.1028
							0.0754
							0.0937

Since $0.3203 < 0.3286 < 0.3511$, the ranking of three SWAs on the basis of quality is: $SWA_y < SWA_x < SWA_z$.

Users may visualize the contribution of each quality attribute to the quality of a SWA; moreover, they may draw contrast in different SWAs through radar charts supported by the AHP procedure of SWAQ. For instance, one may notice in Fig. 3.3 that the three SWAs differ in terms of their SWAQ attributes' values.

SWA_x is the best in terms of scalability (S), while it is the worst in terms of provenance (P). Hence, SWA_x is apt to serve growing number of customers and large openly available data, where P may not be important, such as in the entertainment domain. Due to low value of P, SWA_x is not suitable for the scientific domain. SWA_y has poor functionality and usability and thus needs to be improved first; however, users may be happy about it being authentic and highly available. SWA_y is a decent contender for the scientific domain where maintainability and scalability may be low priority needs, whereas functionality and authenticity of data may be of great significance.

Table 3.9 Overall SWAQ for SWAs

SWA	Product
SWA_x	0.3286
SWA_y	0.3203
SWA_z	0.3511

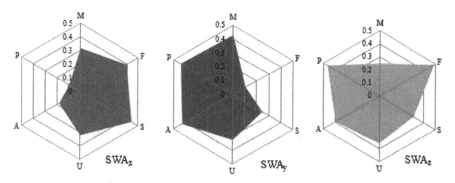

Fig. 3.3 Radar charts for SWAs

3.3.2 Quality-Based Ranking Using Fuzzy Inference System

Fuzzy logic supports multiple intermediate values for attributes, rather than restricting them to yes or no type of extreme values (Jang and Gulley 1995).

Since the SWA quality attributes and sub-attributes are complex to categorize as high valued or low valued, it seems correct to include fuzzy logic in their measures. This permits the allocation of non-numeric values to these attributes. In order to realize a Fuzzy Inference System (FIS), we need to represent the input classes as fuzzy sets, which in turn are represented using membership functions (MFs).

A MF is "a curve that determines how each point in the input space is mapped to a membership value (or degree of membership) between 0 and 1" (Jang and Gulley 1995).

In our case study, we apply the Triangular MF (TMF) owing to its simplicity and wide use by researchers for estimation problems. Moreover, in the absence of a priori knowledge about the MF shape, TMF is easy to use and quick at computation (Jang and Gulley 1995). We assign membership values based on intuition method. A Mamdani-type FIS is opted as it is commonly used by researchers (Mathworks 2014). Additionally, for defuzzification in our example, the centroid method (Jang and Gulley 1995) has been used. The primary idea of a FIS is fuzzification of discrete inputs and defuzzification of fuzzy outputs. The implementation of FIS component of the SWAQ framework consists of the steps mentioned below.

- Fuzzification of inputs, i.e., designing of membership functions;
- Construction of FIS with rule-base based on the expertise of decision maker;
- Application of rule-base on fuzzy inputs (quality attributes), and fuzzy output;
- Defuzzification to transform fuzzy output (SWA quality) to discrete output.

The SWAQ attributes evaluate SWA quality in a unified rather than isolated manner. Hence, fuzzy logic is well suited for tackling ambiguities in the inputted quality values. In the beginning, the range and MFs are decided for inputs and the output. For the fuzzification of inputs, three MFs are opted—Low, Medium, and High. The output 'quality' has five MFs: Very Low, Low, Medium, High, and Very High.

Table 3.10 Sample rules for FIS

Rule	M	F	S	U	A	P	Resultant using SWAQ
3	Low	Low	Low	Low	Low	High	Low
4	Low	Low	Low	Low	Medium	Low	Very Low
...	...	...	...	...	...	...	...
353	Medium	Medium	Medium	Low	Low	Medium	Low
354	Medium	Medium	Medium	Low	Low	High	Medium
...	...	...	...	...	...	...	...
726	High	High	High	High	Medium	High	Very High
727	High	High	High	High	High	Low	High

The partial rule-base is shown in Table 3.10. All rules are fed into the rule-base. According to the input set, a unique rule will be fired, since at a given time only one of the rules has a match by the disjunction method, while all six input values jointly determine the output, i.e., SWA quality by the conjunction method (Jang and Gulley 1995).

Table 3.11 describes the inference engine for FIS. A total of 729 (i.e., 3^6) combinations are possible if we consider all three values (Low, Medium, and High) of each of the six inputs (M, F, S, U, A, P). All rules are fed into the rule-base. Depending on a particular set of inputs, a unique rule is fired. This is because at a given time, only one of the rules has a good match by disjunction method, whereas all six input values collectively decide the output, i.e., SWA quality by the conjunction method. The output, SWA quality, is obtained using MATLAB fuzzy toolbox (Matlab 2017). In our case study, the discrete values of Table 3.6 are inputted to the FIS. It is observed that the overall quality of $SWA_x = 0.43$, $SWA_y = 0.41$, and $SWA_z = 0.52$ is shown in partial view of the rule viewer in Fig. 3.4a–c.

The increasing order of quality of SWAs is $SWA_y < SWA_x < SWA_z$, which is the same as that obtained from AHP in Sect. 3.3.1. This establishes consistency between the results of AHP and FIS components of SWAQ framework.

3.4 Validation

In this section, we validate SWAQ metrics with the help of IEEE Standard 1061 (IEEE 1998) as well as Kitchenham's framework (Kitchenham and Pfleeger 1996).

IEEE Standard 1061 criteria (IEEE 1998)

Criterion: Correlation, i.e., the deviation in a quality attribute's value may be justified by the deviation in its metric. This criterion judges if there is an adequately strong

Table 3.11 Description of Fuzzy Inference System

System Name = 'SWAQ'	Type = 'mamdani', NumInputs = 6 NumOutputs = 1, NumRules = 729 AndMethod = 'min, OrMethod = 'max', ImpMethod = 'min', AggMethod = 'max' DefuzzMethod = 'centroid'
Input	Range = [0 1] NumMFs = 3
Input1-Name = 'M' Input2-Name = 'F' Input3-Name = 'S' Input4-Name = 'U' Input5-Name = 'A' Input6-Name = 'P'	MF1 = 'low':'trimf', [0 0.15 0.4] MF2 = 'medium':'trimf', [0.25 0.5 0.75] MF3 = 'high':'trimf', [0.6 0.85 1]
Output1-Name = 'Quality'	Range = [0 1] NumMFs = 5 MF1 = 'medium':'trimf', [0.35 0.5 0.65] MF2 = 'low':'trimf', [0.2 0.3 0.4] MF3 = 'veryhigh':'trimf', [0.75 0.875 1] MF4 = 'verylow':'trimf', [0 0.15 0.3] MF5 = 'high':'trimf', [0.55 0.7 0.85]

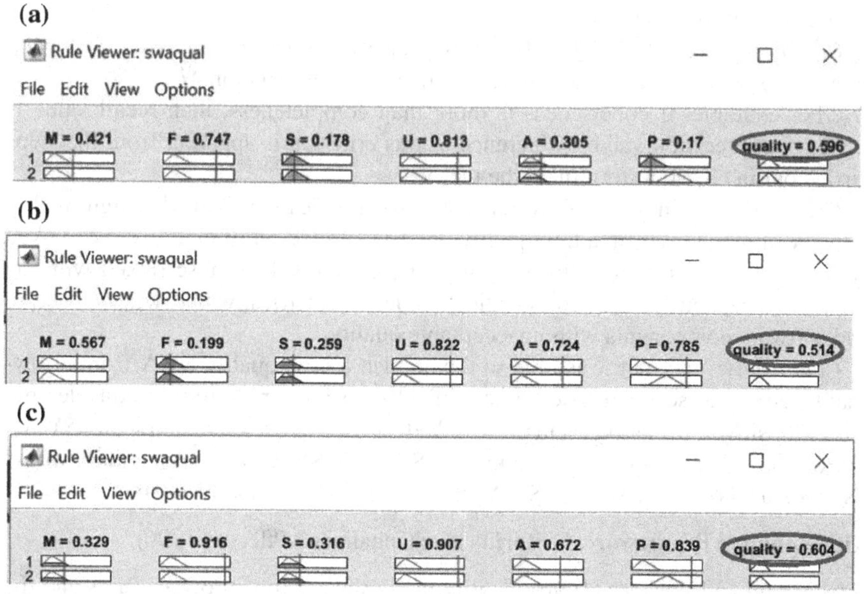

(a)

(b)

(c)

Fig. 3.4 Partial rule viewers for **a** SWA_x, **b** SWA_y, **c** SWA_z

linear relationship between a quality attribute and metric, to license the use of metric in lieu of the quality attribute, whenever it is infeasible to use the latter.

Conformity: The SWAQ metrics may be mapped to quality attributes, through GQM. Thus, there is a strong linear relationship between quality attributes and their metrics; e.g., if the performance in terms of query response time of SWA is poor, the overall quality will be negatively affected.

Criterion: Tracking, i.e., if a metric M is directly proportional to a quality attribute Q, for a given product or process, then a Q_{T1} to Q_{T2} transit from time T_1 to T_2 is coupled with a M_{T1} to M_{T2} transit. This variation follows one direction (i.e., when Q increases, M increases). Further, if M is inversely related to Q, then a variation in Q is coupled with a variation in M in the reverse direction (i.e., if Q increases, M decreases).

Conformity: The SWAQ metrics are calculable either directly (at a point in time) or indirectly (through mathematical formulae), or they are subjective yet quantifiable through AHP. Additionally, all quality attributes barring maintainability are directly linked to quality.

Criterion: Consistency, i.e., for a given set of software components, this criterion checks if the ranks of quality attribute values and that of metrics agree or not. Therefore, consistency determines whether a metric can accurately rank, by quality, a set of products or processes.

Conformity: If attributes $Q_1, Q_2, \ldots, Q_n$ have an association $Q_1 > Q_2 > \cdots Q_n$, then the respective metrics $M_1, M_2, \ldots, M_n$ have an association $M_1 > M_2 > \cdots > M_n$. For example, if conciseness is more than completeness, then recall value is higher than precision value. Adherence to this criterion is apparent from the steps carried out in GQM, to formulate the metrics.

Criterion: Discriminative Power, i.e., a metric is able to distinguish a high-quality software component from a low-quality one because the set of metric values linked to the former would be considerably higher (or lower) than those linked with the latter. This capability recognizes critical values for metrics, which will be used to find software components with unacceptable quality.

Conformity: The metric is able to distinguish a high-quality SWA from a low-quality one. The set of metric values linked with former should be considerably higher (positive correlation) than those linked with the latter. For example, for SWA_x, SWA_y, and SWA_z, with relative ranking as $SWA_x < SWA_z < SWA_y$, quality would also rank as $SWA_x < SWA_z < SWA_y$ if all other factors remain constant.

Kitchenham's Framework Criteria (Kitchenham and Pfleeger 1996)

Kitchenham and Pfleeger (1996) identify the basic constituent of measures and the measurement process. Their framework is widely used for software measurement validation by practitioners and researchers.

Criterion: Attribute Validity, i.e., whether the value of attribute of interest is actually expressed by the entity is measured.

Conformity: SWAQ attributes are exhibited by SWA as generic software features, Web application features, or specific SWA features. These have been derived from the literature.

Criterion: Unit Validity, i.e., whether the unit of measurement is correct or not.

Conformity: AHP uses ratio scale of measurement, making the quality attributes homogeneous. Hence, all units are valid and consistent.

Criterion: Instrument Validity, i.e., whether all models core to the measuring instrument are valid and the measurement process is properly standardized or not.

Conformity: Direct metrics as well as indirect metrics such as usability may be mapped to mathematical formulae. AHP has at its core, pairwise comparisons rather than sorting, electing, or random allotment of precedence.

Criterion: Protocol Validity, i.e., whether a proper measurement convention is adopted or not.

Conformity: The SWAQ attributes borrowed from software and Web applications derive their metric formulations from established models, whereas SWAQ attributes borrowed from SWAs follow GQM as the measurement protocol.

Criterion: Relative Strength, i.e., whether relative strength is taken cared of or not.

Conformity: Relative strength is handled through pairwise weighing in AHP.

Criterion: Dimensionally Consistent, i.e., whether the assimilation of various measures into a compound measure is carried out using a technically comprehendible mathematical function.

Conformity: Elementary Measures, i.e., measures that are not contained in others as sub-measures have been handled carefully. Also, the inclusion of indirect measures may be backed by the need for the perspective of naïve users.

Criterion: No Unexpected Discontinuities, i.e., there are no sudden discontinuities in the values of attributes; i.e., they are more or less continuous.

Conformity: Each SWAQ metric as well as overall SWAQ value is normalized to lie in (0, 1] with no unexpected discontinuities.

3.5 Implementation

The functioning SWAQ's FIS component is shown by calculating the quality of three SWAs and thereby ranking them, in Sect. 3.3.2. The same goal is accomplished by applying AHP on these SWAs, in Sect. 3.3.1. Moreover, the implementation of AHP component is equipped to incorporate novel high-level quality attributes, i.e., horizontally extensible.

We now compare SWAQ with earlier works for assessing SWA quality. Due to the increasing prevalence of Semantic Web, many researchers have studied the quality of various facets of the SWA, namely quality of linked data, quality of supporting ontology, and quality of user interface or inference engine. As discussed in Chap. 2, although there are numerous works on quality assessment of ontology, yet only a handful (Mendes et al. 2012; Pusnik et al. 2013; Zaveri et al. 2013) examines the overall quality of SWAs and formulates metrics for their quality attributes. Table 3.12 lists some attempts toward quality assessment of SWAs as a whole.

Table 3.12 Related works on quality assessment of SWAs

Study	Objective	Contribution	Shortcoming
Mendes et al. (2012)	To evaluate quality of integrated data against user-defined metrics and data fusion functions	A more complete, consistent, and concise data was obtained than original data	Performance and scalability not up to the mark
Pusnik et al. (2013)	To assess quality of XML schemas	Document-oriented metrics for XML schema that target efficacy at maintenance	Validation is required where the SWA backed by the XML schema would be used
Zaveri et al. (2013)	To assess Semantic Web technologies through a model	Semantic Web technology quality model may be applied to Web application for recommendation of semantic technology	The method may be hybridized with a top-down approach to become more comprehensive

Researchers give a detailed review of data quality assessment approaches for Linked Open Data (Zaveri et al. 2013), whereas SWAQ monitors data quality through provenance. The assessment and relative ordering among options are a known concept for Web and cloud services (Baliyan and Kumar 2013b; Garg et al. 2013). However, the evaluation of SWAs through AHP is a new idea (Radulovic and Castro 2011). SWAQ offers a first of its kind metrics suite after identifying key quality attributes.

The implementation of SWAQ could be used in SWA selection based on quality. SWAQ caters to a variety of SWAs, namely data stores such as DBpedia, Freebase; computational search engine such as Wolfram Alpha; and domain-specific applications such as TripIt, BBC Music. SWAQ is extensible to incorporate domain-specific features and omit the rest. For example, a Semantic Web search database such as Freebase may be compared with a similar engine called Twine, but not with the BBC News Web site. Similarly, DuckDuckGo can be compared to Wolfram Alpha (Baliyan and Kumar 2018). Thus, SWAQ facilitates the ranking of SWA alternatives in a specific domain; moreover, the quality of an individual SWA in any domain may be calculated with SWAQ.

3.6   Conclusion and Summary

In this chapter, a framework for Semantic Web application quality assessment (SWAQ) is presented. The methodology for expressing relevant quality metrics derives from the GQM approach, with the facility for precedence among attributes. The precedence indicates user's preference of a SWA attribute to another, in terms of significance. SWAQ is an adaptation of standard software and Web application quality assessment methods and uses ratio scale of measurement. The attributes which are not applicable to a SWA are designated null values for their metrics. The total quality is calculated in a semi-automated way and may be used as a guideline for quality improvement or for specifying non-functional requirements of a SWA. After SWA's deployment, users may verify adherence of metric values to those documented in the requirements. SWAQ's working has been demonstrated for some sample Semantic Web applications, and its validation has been carried out using standard benchmarks. A comparative analysis with related works is also given. The key shortcomings of SWAQ framework are related to user's participation, such as:

- The quality of SWA can only be evaluated if users' discernments can be collected, which usually is not an easy task.
- The performance of the model could be upgraded if user profiles are used while obtaining quality ratings. In this manner, one could depict custom-made and high-quality information, as desired on the current Web.
- The discovery of accurate correlations between data and process quality, with an emphasis on the experiential validation of the models, is desirable.
- There is a lack of development tools to make SWAQ viable.

As part of our future work, we will explore the potential for extension of SWAQ by adding new metrics, data quality rules, and dimensions. Moreover, SWAQ may support semantic data quality improvement by providing transparency in data quality.

To sum up, this chapter provides a framework for quality assessment of SWAs, in totality. However, if such applications are deployed as services on cloud, then the framework needs to be enriched to accommodate more quality attributes due to SWA's delivery as a service. The next chapter tries to address this issue.

References

Abrahao, S., Oscar, P.: Measuring the functional size of web applications. Int. J. Web Eng. Technol. 1(1), 5–16 (2003)

Azuma, M.: SQuaRE: the next generation of the ISO/IEC 9126 and 14598 international standards series on software product quality. In: Proceedings of the European Software Control and Metrics Conference, pp. 337–346 (2001)

Baliyan, N., Kumar, S.: Adaptation of software engineering to semantic web based system development. In: 2013 International Conference on Emerging Trends in Communication, Control, Signal Processing & Computing Applications (C2SPCA), pp. 1–5. IEEE (2013a, October)

Baliyan, N., Kumar, S.; Quality assessment of software as a service on cloud using fuzzy logic. In: 2013 IEEE International Conference on Cloud Computing in Emerging Markets (CCEM), pp. 1–6. IEEE (2013b, October)

Baliyan, N., Kumar, S.: Software process and quality evaluation for semantic web applications. IETE Tech. Rev. 31(6), 452–462 (2014)

Baliyan, N., Kumar, S.: SWAQ: A semantic web application quality evaluation framework. J. Exp. Theor. Artif. Intell. [accepted for publication] (2018)

Barksdale Jr., J.B.: Sets and Randolph Diagrams. Available online at https://files.eric.ed.gov/fulltext/ED045458.pdf. Last accessed Jan 2018 (October 1970)

Bernstein, A.: Software Engineering and the Semantic Web: A Match made in Heaven or in Hell? Software Language Engineering, pp. 203–205. Springer (2011)

Calero, C., Ruiz, J., Piattini, M.: Classifying web metrics using the web quality model. Online Inf. Rev. **29**(3), 227–248 (2005)

Coleman, D., Ash, D., Lowther, B., Oman, P.: Using metrics to evaluate software system maintainability. IEEE Comput. **27**(8), 44–49 (1998)

Garg, S.K., Versteeg, S., Buyya, R.: A framework for ranking of cloud computing services. Future Gener. Comput. Syst. Elsevier **29**(4), 1012–1023 (2013)

HLWIKI.: Semantic Search: HLWIKI International. http://hlwiki.slais.ubc.ca/index.php/Semantic_search. Last modified 13 Aug 2015

IEEE, IEEE STD 1061-1998.: IEEE Standard for a Software Quality Metrics Methodology. http://ieeexplore.ieee.org/xpl/articleDetails.jsp?arnumber=749159 (1998)

Jang, R., Gulley, N.: Fuzzy Logic Toolbox for MATLAB: User's Guide. The Math Works Inc., USA (1995)

Kitchenham, B., Pfleeger, S.L.: Software quality: the elusive target [special issues section]. IEEE Softw. **13**(1), 12–21 (1996)

Koch,R.: The 80/20 Principle: Living the 80/20 Way. Nicholas Brealey Publication (2004)

Marsico, M., Levialdi, S.: Evaluating web sites: exploiting user's expectations. Int. J. Hum. Comput. Stud. **60**(3), 381–416 (2004)

Mathworks.: Comparison of Sugeno and Mamdani Systems. http://www.mathworks.in/help/fuzzy/comparison-of-sugeno-and-mamdani-systems.html. Accessed 12 Aug 2014

Matlab.: Available online at https://www.mathworks.com/products/fuzzy-logic.html. Last accessed Jan 2017

Mendes, P.N., Mühleisen, H., Bizer, C.: Sieve: linked data quality assessment and fusion. In: Proceedings of the Joint EDBT/ICDT Workshops, pp. 116–123 (2012)

Mich, L., Franch, M., Inverardi, P.N.: Choosing the "Rightweight" model for web site quality evaluation. In: Proceedings of Web Engineering, pp. 334–337. Springer, Berlin, Heidelberg (2003)

Pressman, R.S.: Software Engineering: A Practitioner's Approach, 6th International ed., p. 388. McGraw-Hill (2001)

Pusnik, M., Šumak, B., Heričko, M.: Redefining software quality metrics to XML schema needs. In: Proceedings of the 2nd Workshop on Software Quality Analysis, Monitoring, Improvement and Applications, p. 87 (2013)

Radulovic, F., Castro, R.G.: Towards a Quality Model for Semantic Technologies, Lecture Notes in Computer Science, vol. 6786, pp. 244–256. Springer, Berlin, Heidelberg (2011)

Saaty, T.L.: Fundamentals of Decision Making and Priority Theory with the Analytic Hierarchy Process, vol. 6. RWS Publications (2000)

Saaty, T.L.: Decision making with the analytic hierarchy process. Int. J. Serv. Sci. **1**(1), 83–98 (2008)

Signore, O.: A comprehensive model for web sites quality. In: Proceedings of the IEEE 7th International Symposium on Web Site Evolution, pp. 30–36 (2005)

Solingen, R.V., Berghout, E.: The Goal/Question/Metric Method: A Practical Guide for Quality Improvement of Software Development, vol. 7. McGraw Hill (1999)

W3C.: W3C Semantic Web Frequently Asked Questions. http://www.w3.org/RDF/FAQ. Accessed 1 Sept 2014

Zaveri, A., Rula, A., Maurino, A.: Quality assessment methodologies for linked open data. Seman Web J. 1–5 (2013)

Zeleny, M.: Multiple Criteria Decision Making (Cochrane, J.L. (ed.)), vol. 25. McGraw-Hill (1982)

Zhou, Z.: Evaluating websites using a practical quality model. M. Phil. thesis, De Montfort Univ., Leicester (2009)

Chapter 4
Quality Evaluation of Semantic Web Application as a Service

Abstract The quality evaluation of Semantic Web applications (SWAs) in isolation is not enough. The future shall see almost all Web applications being deployed on the cloud and available to us as services, facilitating transparency and reusability. The business model of cloud computing provides services on demand, which are paid as per their use. The Software as a Service (SaaS) delivery model of cloud computing segregates provider's ownership from customer's use. Since the concept of quality is crucial to services, therefore, it is plausible to build models for quality assessment of SWAs, which fit in the cloud's SaaS paradigm. Such applications are referred to Semantic Web application as a service (SWAaaS), in the following text. In our knowledge, there are no quality factors, measures, or frameworks for tracking the quality of SWAaaS. The Semantic Web application quality framework described in Chap. 3 is not profusely appropriate for evaluation of SWAaaS, owing to the distinctive natures of Web application and service. Previously, some ways of assessing quality of SWA and SaaS have been invented, a few of which build on quality features from existing software and Web application quality models, whereas some formulate SaaS quality metrics. few works merely present quality attributes in the context of Service Level Agreement (SLA) and Quality of Service (QoS) parameters. Here, the representative quality factors influencing SWAaaS are recognized after the literature review and a Hierarchical Fuzzy System (HFS) has been developed to assess SWAaaS quality. The quality attributes of HFS have been validated using IEEE 1061 framework. Results of experiments show that our HFS handles multiple quality attributes, and may perform quality-based ranking of SWAs available as services. The hierarchical fuzzy quality model discussed here may serve as a beginning point toward an all-inclusive quality model aimed to facilitate a SWAaaS consumer to choose the best quality service among SWAs available as a service on the cloud. Additionally, HFS may act as a directive to SWAaaS provider for the betterment of quality of SWA that is being provided as a service.

Keywords Semantic Web application · Service
Hierarchical fuzzy inference system

© The Author(s) 2018
S. Kumar and N. Baliyan, *Semantic Web-Based Systems*, SpringerBriefs in Computer Science, https://doi.org/10.1007/978-981-10-7700-5_4

Section 4.1 gives a background of SWAs as a Service and the motivation behind current chapter. Section 4.2 presents the hierarchy of quality attributes alongside their metrics for SWAaaS. The HFS and an algorithm to implement the same are also defined in Sect. 4.2. Next, Sect. 4.3 theoretically endorses the HFS-SWAaaS, using IEEE 1061 criteria. Section 4.4 computes quality of a sample SWAaaS using our model. Lastly, conclusions about the chapter and open research issues are listed in Sect. 4.5.

4.1   Background and Motivation

Let us discuss the background of SWAaaS before delving into their quality attributes' hierarchy. The National Institute of Standards and Technology (NIST) lists cloud computing features as:

- 'On-demand self-service;
- Omnipresent network access;
- Resource pooling at any location;
- Fast elasticity;
- Pay according to use' (Mell and Grance 2011).

Various quality models are available for SaaS quality (Lee et al. 2009; Cancian et al. 2010; Garg et al. 2013). The literature review presented in Baliyan and Kumar (2014a, b) reveals that traditional software quality models are either improper or insufficient for Semantic Web applications (SWAs) deployed on cloud, i.e., available as services.

As SWAs are data-rich, they are a suitable candidate for SaaS. Consider a SWA that saves and recovers primary body indexes such as pulse rate, body mass index, age. This SWA has reusable components archived on the cloud and shareable across hospitals by machines. Multiple advantages like automatic detection and configuration, and simple relocation to the cloud render the use and quality evaluation of SWAs as a Service (SWAaaS), desirable. To the end of exploiting the benefits of SWAaaS, this chapter is directed toward defining a quality evaluation framework that suits the characteristics of SWAaaS offerings.

Besides the quality assessment of SWAs as performed in Chap. 3, there is a need to analyze SWA quality in light of their deployment in the cloud. This can be attributed to effectively capture their unique quality characteristics, in addition to SWA quality characteristics. Further, a Hierarchical Fuzzy System (HFS) bears the multiplicity of quality attributes which turns manifold as we move from SWAs to SWAaaS.

The selection of quality attributes is predominantly affected by three criteria: 1. inclusion of quality attributes owing to the aspects of SaaS which are common to SWAaaS, 2. inclusion of quality attributes owing to the unique aspects of SWAs (Ossenbruggen et al. 2009), 3. the features of a Web application deployed as a service.

Some existing works on SaaS quality quantify the quality notwithstanding ambiguity and bias in quality approximation or do not quantify it at all (Cancian et al.

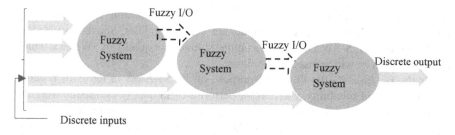

Fig. 4.1 Hierarchical Fuzzy System

2010). However, our SWAaaS quality model has roots in fuzzy logic (Zadeh 1996) and is scalable to include other quality attributes that user chooses. We were motivated to use fuzzy logic due to the innate ambiguity in the estimation of quality attributes' values, besides the bias involved in allocating these values. In his manner, one may call our model an initial step to the end of rule-based modeling of SWAaaS quality criteria.

The chapter is a novel attempt at a practical model that considers an exhaustive list of quality features and evaluates overall SWAaaS quality. The result from our model for a sample input run is a step in the direction of a working fuzzy model for calculation of SWAaaS quality.

Conventional fuzzy systems that are linear in nature have a huge drawback that the cardinality of inputs exponentially affects the cardinality of rules, in a positive direction. With n inputs and m membership functions, such system has m^n rules (Jang and Gulley 1995). This problem is resolved through HFS, comprising multiple atomic fuzzy systems (Lee et al. 2003). The outputs of low-level fuzzy systems are inputted to the high-level fuzzy systems. All rules of the atomic fuzzy systems do not need a redesign; additionally, the rule count is significantly decreased. A visualization of HFS can be seen in Fig. 4.1.

4.2 A Quality Model for SWAaaS

This section discusses the algorithm for HFS, called HFS-SWAaaS. It encompasses the aspect of service deployability into the quality feature of the SWAs available on the cloud. To this end, we feed SWAQ metrics defined in Chap. 3 as inputs for one of the fuzzy systems, whereas additional attributes which determine service quality are accounted for, as well. We start by examining the attributes of a SWA deployed as a service. It encompasses SWA quality attributes and in addition quality attributes of software available as a service, i.e., reliability, accuracy, and suitability (Baliyan and Kumar 2016). The user may assign preference to some aspect of SWAaaS; thus, the model is flexible. The multiplicity of quality attributes (here, 14) in SWAaaS is tackled through our HFS that has five fuzzy systems (fs_0 to fs_4). The number of rules in fuzzy system is significantly reduced from 5^{14} to 5^2 (assuming five membership functions) . The possible values of inputs are Very Poor, Poor, Satisfactory, Good, and Very Good. HFS-SWAaaS offers a unique solution for quality of SWAaaS, which are probable to be widely used in the future.

Firstly, fs_0 assesses the fitness-of-purpose of the SWAaaS in terms of reliability, accuracy, and suitability, whereas fs_1 performs SaaS quality evaluation from the point of view of scalability, transparency, agility, availability, and reusability. Then, fs_2 assesses usability, functionality, scalability, provenance, availability, and maintainability of SWA. Also, the fusion of fs_0 and fs_1 results in fs_3, which assesses the service deployability of SWAaaS. Finally, the merging of fs_2 and fs_3 results in fs_4 which evaluates quality of SWAaaS, in totality. Let us summarize the working of HFS-SWAaaS (Baliyan and Kumar 2016).

A: set of SWAaaS alternatives, $A = \{a_1, a_2, ..., a_n\}$
G: set of measurement sub goals ideated from three aspects- service, SWA, and SaaS
Input: s values
Output: overall SWAaaS quality
1. for each sub goal s, s.t. s ε G,
      get 's to metric' mapping
2. give inputs to each HFS module
      get output by defuzzification.
3. for each a s.t. aε A
      get overall SWAaaS quality from step 2.
4. rank numerous SWAaaS in decreasing order of quality from step 3.
5. if $(rank(a_i) > rank(a_j))$
    Choose a_i
  else
    Choose a_j

The hierarchy of quality attributes as shown in Fig. 4.2 for SWAaaS (Baliyan and Kumar 2016) is built through a comprehensive study and the literature review. Further, either the metrics are formulated from scratch or the available metrics corresponding to each of these attributes are adapted.

The values of fitness-of-purpose and SaaS quality (Baliyan and Kumar 2013) become an intermediary output, service deployability, which along with SWA quality attributes (Chap. 3) act as determinants of the overall SWAaaS quality.

Fig. 4.2 Hierarchical classification of quality aspects of Semantic Web applications as a service

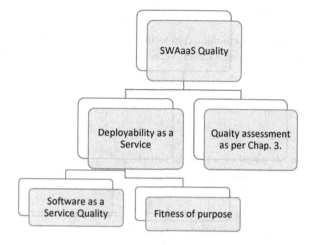

Fitness-of-purpose

One primary requisite for software to be available as a service is to be reliable, accurate, and scalable (Lee et al. 2009). It is only after fulfillment of these requirements that one may evaluate non-functional requirements (Garg et al. 2013). Thus, we discuss the fitness-of-purpose for SWAaaS using these essential features, frequently treated as inherent in a service definition.

Reliability

Reliability measures the ability of the SWAaaS to carry on operating at a particular level of performance over time (Lee et al. 2009). It is defined by (4.1).

$$\text{Reliability} = W_{\text{CFT}} \times \text{CFT} + W_{\text{CFR}} \times \text{CFR} \qquad (4.1)$$

where

CFT	is coverage of fault tolerance
CFR	is coverage of failure recovery
W_{CFT} and W_{CFR}	are weights allocated to CFT and CFR, respectively, defined by (4.2) and (4.3)

$$\text{CFT} = \frac{\text{(Number of faults without becoming failures)}}{\text{(Total number of faults occured)}}. \qquad (4.2)$$

$$\text{CFR} = \frac{\text{(Number of failures remedied)}}{\text{(Total number of failures)}} \qquad (4.3)$$

Accuracy

Accuracy is calculated in terms of the number of times the cloud provider digresses from the Service Level Agreement (Garg et al. 2013) as per (4.4).

$$\text{Accuracy} = \sum_i \frac{\alpha_t - \alpha_i/\alpha_i}{T_i} \qquad (4.4)$$

where

α_t is a unit of service at time t
α_i is a unit of service for ith user
T_i is service time for ith user

Accuracy gauges the level of proximity of user's expected value to the actual value generated from using the service.

Suitability

Suitability is defined as the degree to which a customer's requirements are met by a cloud provider. The value for suitability is represented by (4.5) (Garg et al. 2013).

$$\text{Suitability} = \begin{cases} 1, & \text{if all requests are satisfied} \\ 0, & \text{if no request is satisfied} \\ \dfrac{\text{number of nonfunctional requests provided by service}}{\text{number of nonfunctional requests of the customer}}, & \text{otherwise} \end{cases}$$
$$(4.5)$$

SaaS Quality

Quality attributes for SaaS have been defined by Baliyan and Kumar (2013), along with their quality metrics. At present, a very few quality models principally for SaaS quality are in place, so we read relevant works of quality factors of Web services (Stuckenberg and Heinzl 2010). We even borrowed from contemporary software quality models, whose features are generic enough to be applicable to SaaS (Lee et al. 2009). The motive for short-listing a few representative attributes of SaaS quality is that a few non-redundant measures are more tractable and simpler to manage compared to an exhaustive list of attributes. Baliyan and Kumar (2013) enlist and quantify the attributes used to assess SaaS quality in the novel model as:

- Scalability;
- Transparency;
- Agility;
- Availability;
- Reusability.

Table 4.1 Component fuzzy systems in HFS-SWAaaS

Fuzzy system	Value of various parameters
Fitness-of-purpose (fs_0)	No. of inputs $= 3$, no. of input MFs $= 3$, no. of rules $= 3^3$
SaaS quality (fs_1)	No. of inputs $= 5$, no. of input MFs $= 3$, no. of rules $= 3^5$
SWA quality (fs_2)	No. of inputs $= 6$, no. of input MFs $= 3$, no. of rules $= 3^6$
Service deployability (fs_3)	No. of inputs $= 2$, no. of input MFs $= 5$, no. of rules $= 5^2$
SWAaaS quality (fs_4)	No. of inputs $= 2$, no. of input MFs $= 5$, no. of rules $= 5^2$

SWA Quality

This covers quality attributes of SWAaaS because of machine comprehensible data in it. The SWA quality factors are discussed as SWAQ in Chap. 3. We now define the overall HFS as quality model for SWAaaS and also discuss the MATLAB fuzzy toolbox (Jang and Gulley 1995) implementation of the HFS for SWAaaS. Table 4.1 gives details of component fuzzy systems in our HFS. For each fuzzy system, upon considering all possible values (m) for each input (n), we obtain m^n possible combinations called rules. These rules prepared with the help of domain expert or by logical inference rules are shown in Table 4.2 for top-level fuzzy system. Based on a given set of inputs, single rule will be applicable at a time since exactly one of the rules has a best match by disjunction method, whereas every input value collectively determines the output by the conjunction method (Pedrycz et al. 1993). The output (SWAaaS quality) is attained for a given set of inputs using the MATLAB fuzzy toolbox (Jang and Gulley 1995). The steps in the working of a fuzzy model are: fuzzification of crisp inputs; application of rules from the rule set to obtain fuzzy output; and defuzzification of the fuzzy output.

4.3 Validation

This section evaluates the utility and viability of the HFS-SWAaaS metrics, with the help of IEEE Standard 1061 criteria (IEEE 1998).

Criterion: Correlation, i.e., if the quality factor is linearly related to its metric, strongly enough to guarantee the use of metric as the quality attribute's alternative in case it is not practically possible to employ the latter.

Table 4.2 Complete rule viewer for fs_4

Rule	Inputs		Output
	fs_2	fs_3	fs_4
1	Very poor	Very poor	Very poor
2	Very poor	Poor	Very poor
3	Very poor	Satisfactory	Poor
4	Very poor	Good	Poor
5	Very poor	Very good	Satisfactory
6	Poor	Very poor	Very poor
7	Poor	Poor	Poor
8	Poor	Satisfactory	Poor
9	Poor	Good	Satisfactory
10	Poor	Very good	Good
11	Satisfactory	Very poor	Poor
12	Satisfactory	Poor	Poor
13	Satisfactory	Satisfactory	Satisfactory
14	Satisfactory	Good	Good
15	Satisfactory	Very good	Good
16	Good	Very poor	Poor
17	Good	Poor	Satisfactory
18	Good	Satisfactory	Good
19	Good	Good	Good
20	Good	Very good	Very good
21	Very good	Very poor	Satisfactory
22	Very good	Poor	Good
23	Very good	Satisfactory	Good
24	very good	Good	Very good
25	Very good	Very good	Very good
25	Very good	Very good	Very good

Conformity: The SWAaaS metrics are formularized with the help of the quality attributes' definition or revised from the literature, hence the strong linear association between quality attributes and their metrics.

Criterion: Tracking, i.e., if metric M is directly proportional to quality factor F, then a positive (negative) change in quality factor value from F_{T_1} to F_{T_2} at times T_1 and T_2 is coupled with a positive (negative) change in metric value from M_{T_1} to M_{T_2}. If M is inversely proportional to F, then the variation would be in the inverse direction.

Conformity: The metrics are quantifiable either directly or indirectly. Furthermore, they are directly related to total quality.

Criterion: Consistency: In line with the correlation criterion, the values within quality attributes also possess a strong linear link. This criterion verifies consistency between ranks of quality factor and that of metric values, for given software entity. It decides whether the metric can correctly rank the entity by quality.

Conformity: If attributes $A_1, A_2, \ldots, A_n$ have a relation $A_1 > A_2 > \cdots > A_n$, then corresponding metrics $M_1, M_2, \ldots, M_n$ have the relation $M_1 > M_2 > \cdots > M_n$. Each of the metrics is computed based on numerical values of multiple performance features of SWAaaS; hence, consistency is manifested in the metrics.

Criterion: Discriminative Power, i.e., a metric is capable of discriminating between high-quality and low-quality software entities. The metric values of the former should be considerably larger than those of the latter. Discriminative power recognizes crucial values which further rule out software entities having unacceptable quality.

Conformity: Three SWAaaS with ranking $SWAaaS_x < SWAaaS_z < SWAaaS_y$, for SWAQ attributes rank as $SWAaaS_x < SWAaaS_z < SWAaaS_y$, if the rest of the quality factors (i.e., fitness-of-purpose and SaaS quality) are kept stable.

4.4 Implementation

Here, we demonstrate how a discrete value of SWAaaS quality is obtained through an inclusive rule set. Consider three sample Semantic Web applications as services whose quality metrics are fed to our fuzzy system, as shown in Fig. 4.3a–c.

In $SWAaaS_x$, the service deployability is 0.719, and SWAQ value is 0.662. On applying both inputs to the topmost fuzzy system in hierarchy, conjunction/ANDing gives minimum value of all inputs. Further, when rules are implicated, the output fuzzy value is 0.726. The defuzzification can be achieved by computing the center of gravity (Mathworks 2015) of the fuzzy output. Similar output is obtained through simulation in MATLAB (Fig. 4.4). The resulting crisp value for SWAaaS quality is checked to be lying in *Very Good* range, according to the centroid method for defuzzification, and also by the center of gravity computation. Figure 4.4 shows the surface view of output, i.e., SWAaaS quality.

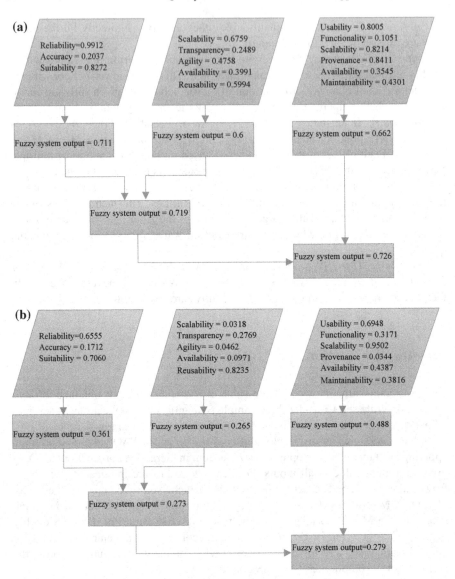

Fig. 4.3 HFS-SWAaaS for: **a** SWAaaS$_x$; **b** SWAaaS$_y$; **c** SWAaaS$_z$

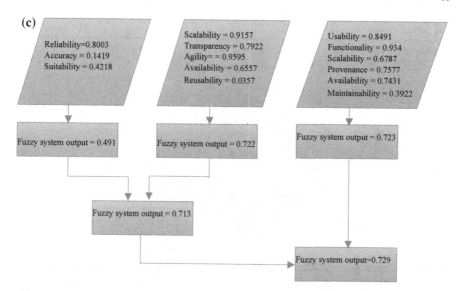

Fig. 4.3 (continued)

4.5 Conclusion and Summary

SWAaaS quality varies from that of the software, owing to the delivery of SWAaaS in service form and the annotation of semantics. The SaaS paradigm of cloud computing makes rich use of reusability and provides services on demand. Thus, the task of observing and bettering the quality of SWAs available as SaaS assumes significance.

This chapter discussed quality metrics for Semantic Web applications deployed as a service, from the aspect of deployability, in addition to semantic capabilities. Our quality model shows positive association of different arrangements of the fourteen quality attributes identified from the standard literature and the resultant SWAaaS quality. If the value of scalability is low, so is the level of overall SWAaaS quality. Further, the integrated value for quality indicates SWAaaS quality better than an isolated measure of quality. Our model may facilitate a cloud user to choose a service as per his/her customized quality comprising desirable quality aspects.

Moreover, the use of fuzzy logic resolves uncertainty and subjectivity involved in estimating quality attributes. The hierarchical fuzzy inference system tackles multiplicity of quality factors and may scale out to encompass more quality attributes. The metrics were validated through IEEE 1061, and a sample computation is also shown. In the future, other soft computing techniques could be explored for quality prediction in SWAaaS.

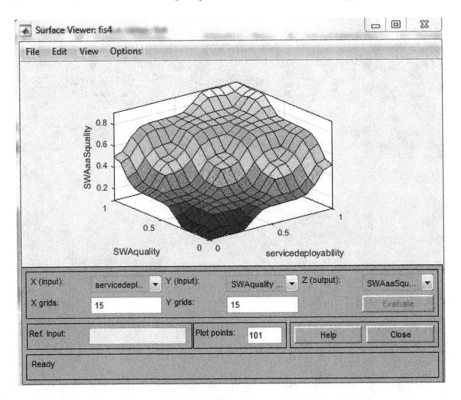

Fig. 4.4 Surface view of the output—SWAaaS quality

References

Baliyan, N., Kumar, S.: Quality assessment of software as a service on cloud using fuzzy logic. In: 2013 IEEE International Conference on Cloud Computing in Emerging Markets (CCEM), pp. 1–6. IEEE (2013)

Baliyan, N., Kumar, S.: Towards software engineering paradigm for software as a service. In: 2014 Seventh International Conference on Contemporary Computing (IC3), pp. 329–333. IEEE (2014a)

Baliyan, N., Kumar, S.: Software process and quality evaluation for semantic web applications. IETE Tech. Rev. **31**(6), 452–462 (2014)

Baliyan, N., Kumar, S.: A hierarchical fuzzy system for quality assessment of semantic web application as a service. ACM SIGSOFT Softw. Eng. Notes **41**(1), 1–7 (2016)

Cancian, M.H., Carlo, J., Hauck, R., von Wangenheim, C.G., Rabelo, R.J.: Discovering software process and product quality criteria in software as a service. In: Product-Focused Software Process Improvement, pp. 234–247. Springer, Berlin Heidelberg (2010)

Garg, S.K., Versteeg, S., Buyya, R.: A framework for ranking of cloud computing services. Future Gener. Comput. Syst. **29**(4), 1012–1023 (2013)

IEEE, IEEE STD 1061-1998: IEEE standard for a software quality metrics methodology. http://ieeexplore.ieee.org/xpl/articleDetails.jsp?arnumber=749159 (1998)

Jang, R., Gulley, N.: Fuzzy logic toolbox for matlab: user's guide. The Math Works Inc., USA (1995)

Lee, J.Y., Lee, J.W., Cheun, D.W., Kim, S.D.: A quality model for evaluating software-as-a-service in cloud computing. In: Proceedings of the ACIS 7th International Conference on Software Engineering Research, Management and Applications, pp. 261–266 (2009)

Lee, M.L., Chung, H.Y., Yu, F.M.: Modeling of hierarchical fuzzy systems. Fuzzy Sets Syst. J. **138**(2), 343–361 (2003)

Mathworks: Foundations of fuzzy logic. http://in.mathworks.com/help/fuzzy/foundations-of-fuzz y-logic.html#bp78l70-2. Accessed 12 May 2015

Mell, P., Grance, T.: The NIST definition of cloud computing recommendations of the National Institute of Standards and Technology. NIST Specification Publication **145**(1), 1–7 (2011)

Ossenbruggen, J.V., Amin, A., Hildebrand. M.: Why evaluating semantic web applications is difficult. In: Proceedings of the CEUR Workshop, vol. 543 (2009)

Pedrycz, W.: Fuzzy Control and Fuzzy Systems. Wiley (1993)

Stuckenberg, S., Heinzl, A: The impact of the software-as-a-service concept on the underlying software and service development processes. In: Proceedings of the PACIS Conference, p. 125 (2010)

Zadeh, L.A.: Fuzzy logic = computing with words. IEEE Trans. Fuzzy Syst. **4**(2), 103–111 (1996)

Closing Remarks

The material presented in this book is mix of basic topics and research works published at various venues. This book mainly provides summary of information available in public domain on the topic of quality assessment of Semantic Web-based systems and provides easy pointers to the corresponding detailed documents. This book also includes the summary of various published works by the authors and their other team members who have worked with them previously. It is authors' expectation that readers will find this book easy to read and understand. Various tables and figures will also help in betterment of reading experience. Efforts have been done to create better connectivity of various chapters to increase interest of readers.

© The Author(s) 2018   89
S. Kumar and N. Baliyan, *Semantic Web-Based Systems*, SpringerBriefs in Computer
Science, https://doi.org/10.1007/978-981-10-7700-5

Index

© The Author(s) 2018
S. Kumar and N. Baliyan, *Semantic Web-Based Systems*, SpringerBriefs in Computer
Science, https://doi.org/10.1007/978-981-10-7700-5

Printed in the United States
By Bookmasters